JAMES

Guidelines for a Happy Christian Life

JOHN MACARTHUR

THOMAS NELSON
Since 1798

JAMES
MACARTHUR BIBLE STUDIES

© 2007, John MacArthur

Published in Nashville, Tennessee, by Nelson Books, an imprint of Thomas Nelson. Nelson Books and Thomas Nelson are registered trademarks of HarperCollins Christian Publishing, Inc.

Nelson Books titles may be purchased in bulk for education, business, fundraising, or sales promotional use. For information, please email SpecialMarkets@ThomasNelson.com.

Published in association with the literary agency of Wolgemuth & Associates, Inc.

Produced with the assistance of the Livingstone Corporation. Project staff include Jake Barton, Betsy Todt Schmitt, and Andy Culbertson. Project editors: Mary Horner Collins, Amber Rae, and Len Woods.

Cover Art by Holly Sharp Design
Interior Design and Composition by Joel Bartlett, Livingstone Corporation

ISBN: 978-0-7180-3516-7

First Printing April 2016 / Printed in the United States of America

CONTENTS

INTRODUCTION TO JAMES

James, like all the general epistles except Hebrews, is named after its author (v. 1).

AUTHOR AND DATE

Of the four men named James in the New Testament, only two are candidates for authorship of this epistle. No one has seriously considered James the Less, the son of Alphaeus (Matt. 10:3; Acts 1:13), or James the father of Judas, not Iscariot (Luke 6:16; Acts 1:13). Some have suggested James the son of Zebedee and brother of John (Matt. 4:21), but he was martyred too early to have written it (Acts 12:2). That leaves only James the oldest half brother of Christ and brother of Jude (Matt. 13:55; Mark 6:3; Jude 1). James had at first rejected Jesus as Messiah (John 7:5), but later believed (1 Cor. 15:7). He became the key leader in the Jerusalem church (see Acts 12:17; 15:13; 21:18; Gal. 2:12), being called one of the "pillars" of that church, along with Peter and John (Gal. 2:9). Also known as James the Just because of his devotion to righteousness, he was martyred ca. AD 62, according to the first-century Jewish historian Josephus. A comparison of James's vocabulary in his letter recorded in Acts 15 with that in the epistle of James further corroborates his authorship.

James		Acts 15
1:1	"greetings"	15:23
1:16, 19; 2:5	"beloved"	15:25
1:21; 5:20	"your souls"	15:24
1:27	"visit"	15:14
2:10	"keep"	15:24
5:19–20	"turn"	15:19

James wrote with the authority of one who had personally seen the resurrected Christ (1 Cor. 15:7), who was recognized as an associate of the apostles (Gal. 1:19), and who was the leader of the Jerusalem church.

James most likely wrote this epistle to believers scattered abroad as a result of the unrest recorded in Acts 12 (ca. AD 44). There is no mention of the Council of Jerusalem described in Acts 15 (ca. AD 49), which would be expected if that Council had already taken place. Therefore, James can be reliably dated ca. AD 44–49, making it the earliest written book of the New Testament canon.

Background and Setting

The recipients of this book were Jewish believers who had been dispersed, possibly as a result of Stephen's martyrdom (Acts 7, AD 31–34), but more likely due to the persecution under Herod Agrippa I (Acts 12, ca. AD 44). The author refers to his audience as "brethren" fifteen times (1:2, 16, 19; 2:1, 5, 14; 3:1, 10, 12; 4:11; 5:7, 9, 10, 12, 19); this was a common epithet among first-century Jews. Not surprisingly, then, James is Jewish in its content. For example, the Greek word translated "assembly" (2:2) is the word for "synagogue." Further, James contains more than forty allusions to the Old Testament (and more than twenty to the Sermon on the Mount, Matt. 5–7).

Historical and Theological Themes

James, with its devotion to direct, pungent statements on wise living, is reminiscent of the book of Proverbs. It has a practical emphasis, stressing not theoretical knowledge but godly behavior. James wrote with a passionate desire for his readers to be uncompromisingly obedient to the Word of God. He uses at least thirty references to nature (e.g., "wave of the sea" [1:6]; "reptile" [3:7]; and "heaven gave rain" [5:18]), as befits one who spent a great deal of time outdoors. He complements Paul's emphasis on justification by faith with his own emphasis on spiritual fruitfulness demonstrating true faith.

Interpretive Challenges

At least two significant texts challenge the interpreter: (1) In 2:14–26, what is the relationship between faith and works? Does James's emphasis on works contradict Paul's focus on faith? (2) In 5:13–18, do the promises of healing refer to the spiritual or the physical realm? These difficult texts are treated in the notes for those chapters.

FROM TROUBLE TO TRIUMPH
James 1:1–12

DRAWING NEAR

James opens his book by emphasizing the reality of hard times. How do you usually respond to trials or setbacks in your life? Why?

Describe a situation in which a Christian you know has handled a difficult trial with exceptional grace and humility. What do you think made the difference? What was his or her "secret"?

What do you want to learn in this study? Ask God to open your heart and mind to be receptive to the no-nonsense approach to living out your faith.

THE CONTEXT

James's major emphasis in this section of his epistle is this: If a person's faith is genuine, it will prove itself during times of trouble, whatever the nature or source of the trouble may be.

The clear message of Scripture is that trials are a tool in the loving hands of the Lord. They test the strength of our faith; they humble us; they wean us from our dependence on earthly things; they call us to eternal and heavenly hope; they reveal what we really love; they teach us to value God's blessings; they develop enduring strength for greater usefulness; they help us better encourage others who are in times of trial.

Since trials are so productive, it is essential for us to respond rightly to them. James helps us greatly in this by giving five means for persevering through trials. He then tells us of the reward for perseverance.

Keys to the Text

Jewish Diaspora: James wrote to Christian Jews living in the Roman Empire, who had been "scattered abroad" because of persecution. The word "scattered" is from the Greek word *diaspora*, which literally means "through a sowing" (see John 7:35). Thus, the "diaspora" became a technical term referring to Jews living outside the land of Palestine. In the Old Testament, Jews were expelled from the land by the Assyrians (2 Kings 17; 1 Chron. 5) and Babylonians (2 Kings 24–25; 2 Chron. 36). The majority of Israelites did not return to Judea after the Exile. The geographical movement of Israelites continued in the Greek and Roman Empires so that by the first century AD, Jews were found throughout the Mediterranean basin and Mesopotamia. But James's primary audience was those who were scattered because of current persecution, some of whom were once led by a Jew named Saul of Tarsus (see Acts 8:1).

Trials: This Greek word connotes trouble, or something that breaks the pattern of peace, comfort, joy, and happiness in someone's life. The verb form of this word means "to put someone or something to the test," with the purpose of discovering that person's nature or that thing's quality. God brings such tests to prove—and increase—the strength and quality of one's faith and to demonstrate its validity (vv. 2–12). Every trial becomes a test of faith designed to strengthen; if the believer fails the test by responding wrongly, that test then becomes a temptation or a solicitation to evil.

Unleashing the Text

Read James 1:1–12, noting the key words and definitions next to the passage.

James (v. 1)—the half brother of the Lord Jesus (see Introduction)

twelve tribes (v. 1)—a common New Testament title for Jews.

James 1:1–12 (NKJV)

1 *James, a bondservant of God and of the Lord Jesus Christ, to the twelve tribes which are scattered abroad: Greetings.*

When the kingdom split after Solomon's reign, ten tribes constituted the northern kingdom, called Israel, and Benjamin and Judah combined to form the southern kingdom, called Judah. After the fall and deportation of the northern kingdom to Assyria (722 BC), some of the remnant of those in the ten northern tribes filtered down into Judah and came to Jerusalem to worship (2 Chron. 29, 30, 34), thus preserving all twelve tribes in Judah's land. Although tribal identity could not be established with certainty after the southern kingdom was led captive by Babylon (586 BC), the prophets foresaw a time

2 *My brethren, count it all joy when you fall into various trials,*

3 *knowing that the testing of your faith produces patience.*

4 *But let patience have its perfect work, that you may be perfect and complete, lacking nothing.*

5 *If any of you lacks wisdom, let him ask of God, who gives to all liberally and without reproach, and it will be given to him.*

6 *But let him ask in faith, with no doubting, for he who doubts is like a wave of the sea driven and tossed by the wind.*

7 *For let not that man suppose that he will receive anything from the Lord;*

8 *he is a double-minded man, unstable in all his ways.*

9 *Let the lowly brother glory in his exaltation,*

when God would reconstitute the whole nation and delineate each person's tribal membership once again (see Isa. 11:12–13; Jer. 3:18; 50:4; Rev. 7:5–8).

brethren (v. 2)—believing Jews among those scattered

count it all joy (v. 2)—The Greek word for *count* may also be translated "consider" or "evaluate." The natural human response to trials is not to rejoice; therefore the believer must make a conscious commitment to face them with joy.

testing (v. 3)—This means "proof" or "proving."

patience (v. 3)—better translated "endurance" or "perseverance"; through tests, a Christian will learn to withstand tenaciously the pressure of a trial until God removes it at His appointed time, at which point he will even cherish the benefit.

perfect (v. 4)—not a reference to sinless perfection (see 3:2), but rather to spiritual maturity; the testing of faith drives believers to deeper communion and greater trust in Christ—qualities that in turn produce a stable, godly, and righteous character

complete (v. 4)—from a compound Greek word that literally means "all the portions whole"

wisdom (v. 5)—James's Jewish audience recognized this as the understanding and practical skill that was necessary to live life to God's glory. It was not a wisdom of philosophical speculation, but the wisdom contained in the pure and peaceable absolutes of God's will revealed in His Word (see 3:13, 17) and lived out. Only such divine wisdom enables believers to be joyous and submissive in the trials of life.

ask of God (v. 5)—This command is a necessary part of the believer's prayer life. God intends that trials will drive believers to greater dependency on Him, by showing them their own inadequacy. As with all His riches (Eph. 1:7; 2:7; 3:8; Phil. 4:19), God has wisdom in abundance available for those who seek it.

ask in faith (v. 6)—Prayer must be offered with confident trust in a sovereign God.

with no doubting (v. 6)—This refers to having one's thinking divided within himself, not merely because of mental indecision but an inner moral conflict or distrust in God.

wave of the sea (v. 6)—The person who doubts God's ability or willingness to provide this wisdom is like the billowing, restless sea, moving back and forth with its endless tides, never able to settle.

double-minded man (v. 8)—a literal translation of the Greek expression that denotes having one's mind or soul divided between God and the world; this man is a hypocrite, who occasionally believes in God but fails to trust Him when trials come and thus receives nothing; the use of this expression in 4:8 makes it clear that it refers to an unbeliever

lowly brother . . . the rich (vv. 9–10)—Trials make all believers equally dependent on God and bring them to the same level with each other by keeping them from becoming preoccupied with earthly things. Poor Christians and wealthy ones alike can rejoice that God is no respecter of persons and that they both have the privilege of being identified with Christ.

glory (v. 9)—This word refers to the boasting of a privilege or possession; it is the joy of legitimate pride. Although having nothing in this world, the poor believer can rejoice in his high spiritual standing before God by grace.

5

his humiliation (v. 10)—refers to the rich believer's being brought low by trials; such experiences help him rejoice and realize that genuine happiness and contentment depend on the true riches of God's grace, not earthly wealth.

grass ... flower (v. 11)—This pictures Palestine's flowers and flowering grasses, which colorfully flourish in February and dry up by May; it is a clear allusion to Isaiah 40:6–8, which speaks of the scorching sirocco wind that burns and destroys plants in its path. This picture from nature illustrates how divinely wrought death and judgment can quickly end the wealthy person's dependence on material possessions.

10 *but the rich in his humiliation, because as a flower of the field he will pass away.*

11 *For no sooner has the sun risen with a burning heat than it withers the grass; its flower falls, and its beautiful appearance perishes. So the rich man also will fade away in his pursuits.*

12 *Blessed is the man who endures temptation; for when he has been approved, he will receive the crown of life which the Lord has promised to those who love Him.*

Blessed (v. 12)—Believers who successfully endure trials are truly happy (see 5:11).

endures (v. 12)—In this context, it also describes the passive, painful survival of a trial and focuses on the victorious outcome. Such a person never relinquishes his saving faith in God; thus this concept is closely related to the doctrine of eternal security and perseverance of the believer (see John 14:15, 23; 1 John 2:5–6, 15, 19; 1 Pet. 1:6–8).

temptation (v. 12)—This is better translated "trials."

approved (v. 12)—literally "passed the test." The believer has successfully and victoriously gone through his trials, indicating he is genuine because his faith has endured like Job's.

crown of life (v. 12)—best translated "the crown which is life." "Crown" was the wreath put on the victor's head after ancient Greek athletic events; here it denotes the believer's ultimate reward—eternal life—which God has promised to him and will grant in full at death or at Christ's coming.

1) What do you learn about the recipients of James's letter?

_____

_____

_____

_____

2) What can trials accomplish in the life of a believer?

_____

_____

_____

_____

(Verses to consider: 2 Cor. 12:7–10; 1 Pet. 5:10)

3) According to James, how should believers respond to trials? What part does wisdom play?

_____

_____

_____

_____

_____

(Verses to consider: Prov. 3:5–7; Acts 5:40–42; 1 Thess. 5:16–18; Heb. 12:2–3)

4) What does it mean to be double-minded? Give an example, if you can.

_____

_____

_____

_____

_____

5) How do trials act as an equalizer to the rich and the poor?

_____

_____

_____

_____

6) What do you learn about the reward God promises for enduring trials and temptation (v. 12)?

_____

_____

_____

_____

GOING DEEPER

For more insight about the value of trials in our lives, read what the apostle Peter wrote in 1 Peter 1:6–9.

> 6 *In this you greatly rejoice, though now for a little while, if need be, you have been grieved by various trials,*
>
> 7 *that the genuineness of your faith, being much more precious than gold that perishes, though it is tested by fire, may be found to praise, honor, and glory at the revelation of Jesus Christ,*
>
> 8 *whom having not seen you love. Though now you do not see Him, yet believing, you rejoice with joy inexpressible and full of glory,*
>
> 9 *receiving the end of your faith—the salvation of your souls.*

EXPLORING THE MEANING

7) In what way do trials prove our faith is genuine? What does that mean?

_____

_____

_____

_____

8) How does having faith in what we have "not seen" make a difference in difficult times?

_____

_____

_____

9) Read Hebrews 11:1, 6. What do these verses say about the role of faith in our dealings with God?

_____

_____

_____

10) Read Proverbs 3:5–6. Compare and contrast this passage with James 1:5–6. What helpful principles about wisdom do you observe?

_____

_____

_____

TRUTH FOR TODAY

To test the genuineness of a diamond, jewelers often place it in clear water, which causes a real diamond to sparkle with special brilliance. An imitation stone, on the other hand, will have almost no sparkle at all. When the two are placed side by side, even an untrained eye can easily tell the difference. In a similar way, the world can often notice the marked differences between genuine Christians and those who merely profess faith in Christ. As with jewels, there is a noticeable difference in radiance, especially when people are undergoing difficult times. Many people have great confidence in their faith until it is severely tested by hardships and disappointments. How a person handles trouble will reveal whether his faith is living or dead, genuine or imitation, saving or non-saving.

REFLECTING ON THE TEXT

11) Is there something in your life that you would call a "trial" or "test"? What makes it hard to be joyful in the midst of that difficulty?

_____

_____

_____

_____

12) How would you define _endurance_ as it relates to the Christian life? According to James 1:12, why is it imperative that we persevere?

_____

_____

_____

_____

(Verses to consider: 2 Tim. 4:8; 1 Pet. 5:4; Rev. 2:10)

13) What difference does it make to know that God is working through trials to build good things in our lives?

_____

_____

_____

_____

14) How can the truths of this lesson help you move from troubles to triumph?

_____

_____

_____

_____

PERSONAL RESPONSE

Write out additional reflections, questions you may have, or a prayer.

_____

_____

_____

_____

_____

_____

_____

_____

_____

_____

_____

_____

_____

2

UNDERSTANDING TEMPTATION
James 1:13–18

DRAWING NEAR

One of the chief characteristics of sin is the propensity to pass the blame.
What are some creative "excuses" you have heard people give for doing
something that is clearly wrong?

_____

_____

_____

_____

_____

Think of a time when you have done something wrong, big or small, and
tried to cover it up. What makes it so hard to own up to our own guilt?

_____

_____

_____

_____

THE CONTEXT

It's human nature to deflect responsibility. We see this from the very beginning
of creation. When God confronted Adam with his sin in the Garden of Eden,
Adam's reply was, "The woman whom You gave to be with me, she gave me from
the tree, and I ate." When the Lord asked Eve, "What is this you have done?" she
replied, "The serpent deceived me, and I ate" (Gen. 3:12–13). Eve blamed Satan.
Adam blamed the woman, but really blamed God. And on it goes today.

So is God ultimately responsible for our temptations and sin? James provides
four strong proofs that God is not responsible for our temptations nor for our
weakness in succumbing to sin. James explains the nature of evil, the nature
of man, the nature of lust, and the nature of God. As you read this passage, be
thankful that through Jesus Christ, God has provided a way for us to be delivered
from our sin natures!

Keys to the Text

Sin: The transgression of God's will in thought, word, or deed. When we were born physically, we inherited from Adam the *flesh* with its propensity to sin. The one word that best characterizes sin—the flesh, our human nature—is *selfish.* The sin of Adam centered on setting his own will and interests against God's; and that has been the center of sin ever since. Jesus made it clear that man's basic problem is not with what is outside of him but with what is within him (see Mark 7:20–23). When we were born spiritually and given a new heart, God broke the back of sin and paid its penalty. But the tendency toward evil desires remains.

Temptation: The Greek word *peirasmos* (the noun form of the verb translated *tempted*) has the basic meaning of trying, testing, assaying, or proving and can have negative or positive connotations, depending on the context. In James 1:12 the word is used in the sense of trials or testings. But in the present text (vv. 13–14), the idea is clearly that of temptation, of solicitation to evil. Here James deals with an entirely different concept, the difference being not in the test itself but in a person's response to it. If a believer responds in faithful obedience to God's Word, he successfully endures a trial; if he succumbs to it in the flesh, doubting God and disobeying, he is tempted to sin. Right response leads to spiritual endurance, righteousness, wisdom, and other blessings. Wrong response leads to sin and death.

Unleashing the Text

Read James 1:13–18, noting the key words and definitions next to the passage.

tempted (v. 13)—The same Greek word translated "trials" (vv. 2–12) is also translated "temptation" here.

God cannot be tempted (v. 13)—God by His holy nature has no capacity for evil or vulnerability to it.

James 1:13–18 (NKJV)

13 *Let no one say when he is tempted, "I am tempted by God"; for God cannot be tempted by evil, nor does He Himself tempt anyone.*

14 *But each one is tempted when he is drawn away by his own desires and enticed.*

nor does He Himself tempt anyone (v. 13)—God purposes trials to occur, and in them He allows temptation to happen, but He has promised not to allow more than believers can endure and never without a way to escape. Believers choose whether to take the escape God provides or to give in.

drawn away (v. 14)—This Greek word was used to describe wild game being lured into traps. Just as animals can be drawn to their deaths by attractive baits, temptation promises people something good, which is actually harmful.

his own desires (v. 14)—This refers to lust, the strong desire of the human soul to enjoy or acquire something to fulfill the flesh. Man's fallen nature has the propensity to strongly desire whatever sin will satisfy it; "his own" describes the individual nature of lust—it is different for each person as a result of

15 *Then, when desire has conceived, it gives birth to sin; and sin, when it is full-grown, brings forth death.*

16 *Do not be deceived, my beloved brethren.*

17 *Every good gift and every perfect gift is from above, and comes down from the Father of lights, with whom there is no variation or shadow of turning.*

18 *Of His own will He brought us forth by the word of truth, that we might be a kind of firstfruits of His creatures.*

inherited tendencies, environment, upbringing, and personal choices. The Greek grammar also indicates that these "desires" are the direct agent or cause of one's sinning.

enticed (v. 14)—a fishing term that means "to capture" or "to catch with bait"; it is a parallel to "drawn away"

has conceived . . . gives birth . . . brings forth (v. 15)—Sin is not merely a spontaneous act, but the result of a process. The Greek words for "has conceived" and "brings forth" liken the process to physical conception and birth; thus James personifies temptation and shows that it can follow a similar sequence and produce sin with all its deadly results. While sin does not result in spiritual death for the believer, it can lead to physical death.

Do not be deceived (v. 16)—The Greek expression refers to erring, going astray, or wandering. Christians are not to make the mistake of blaming God rather than themselves for their sin.

Every good . . . perfect gift is from above (v. 17)—Two different Greek words for "gift" emphasize the perfection and inclusiveness of God's graciousness; the first denotes the act of giving, and the second is the object given. Everything related to divine giving is adequate, complete, and beneficial.

Father of lights (v. 17)—an ancient Jewish expression for God as the Creator, with "lights" referring to the sun, moon, and stars

no variation or shadow of turning (v. 17)—From man's perspective, the celestial bodies have different phases of movement and rotation, change from day to night, and vary in intensity and shadow; but God does not follow that pattern—He is changeless.

Of His own will (v. 18)—This phrase translates a Greek word that makes the point that regeneration is not just a wish, but an active expression of God's will, which He always has the power to accomplish. This phrase occurs at the beginning of the Greek sentence, which means James intends to emphasize that the sovereign will of God is the source of this new life.

He brought us forth (v. 18)—the divine act of regeneration, or the new birth

word of truth (v. 18)—Scripture, or the Word of God; He regenerates sinners through the power of that Word.

firstfruits (v. 18)—originally an Old Testament expression referring to the first and best harvest crops, which God expected as an offering (see Exod. 23:19; Deut. 26:1–19); giving God that initial crop was an act of faith that He would fulfill His promise of a full harvest to come; in the same way, Christians are the first evidence of God's new creation that is to come, and they presently enjoy in their new life a foretaste of future glory

1) What do you learn about God's nature in this passage (vv. 13, 17)?

_____

_____

_____

2) Describe the progression from temptation to sin.

_____

_____

_____

_____

3) James warns the believers not to be deceived. In what ways can we be deceived when it comes to temptation?

_____

_____

_____

_____

4) What does James mean when he says that in God there is "no variation or shadow of turning" (v. 17)?

_____

_____

_____

_____

(Verses to consider: Mal. 3:6; Heb. 13:8)

GOING DEEPER

The apostle Paul wrote about our continuing struggle with sin. Read Romans 7:8–25.

8 *But sin, taking opportunity by the commandment, produced in me all manner of evil desire. For apart from the law sin was dead.*

9 *I was alive once without the law, but when the commandment came, sin revived and I died.*

10 *And the commandment, which was to bring life, I found to bring death.*

11 *For sin, taking occasion by the commandment, deceived me, and by it killed me.*

12 *Therefore the law is holy, and the commandment holy and just and good.*

13 *Has then what is good become death to me? Certainly not! But sin, that it might appear sin, was producing death in me through what is good, so that sin through the commandment might become exceedingly sinful.*

14 *For we know that the law is spiritual, but I am carnal, sold under sin.*

15 *For what I am doing, I do not understand. For what I will to do, that I do not practice; but what I hate, that I do.*

16 *If, then, I do what I will not to do, I agree with the law that it is good.*

17 *But now, it is no longer I who do it, but sin that dwells in me.*

18 *For I know that in me (that is, in my flesh) nothing good dwells; for to will is present with me, but how to perform what is good I do not find.*

19 *For the good that I will to do, I do not do; but the evil I will not to do, that I practice.*

20 *Now if I do what I will not to do, it is no longer I who do it, but sin that dwells in me.*

21 *I find then a law, that evil is present with me, the one who wills to do good.*

22 *For I delight in the law of God according to the inward man.*

23 *But I see another law in my members, warring against the law of my mind, and bringing me into captivity to the law of sin which is in my members.*

24 *O wretched man that I am! Who will deliver me from this body of death?*

25 *I thank God—through Jesus Christ our Lord! So then, with the mind I myself serve the law of God, but with the flesh the law of sin.*

EXPLORING THE MEANING

5) What are the main points Paul makes here about the internal struggle all Christians have between enticement to evil and desire for God-honoring righteous living?

_____

_____

_____

_____

6) How is sin defined in this Romans 7 passage?

_____

_____

_____

_____

7) Read Ephesians 2:5–6. What has God done in the life of each believer that, in effect, gives them no excuse for sin?

_____

_____

_____

_____

(Verses to consider: Ezek. 36:25–27; John 1:12–13)

TRUTH FOR TODAY

When a person becomes a Christian, God gives him a completely new spiritual and moral capability that a mind apart from Christ could never achieve. The new birth results from God's sovereignty coming down to a sinner and by His grace cleansing him, planting His Spirit within him, and giving him a completely new spiritual nature. He then has "put on the new man, which was created according to God, in true righteousness and holiness" (Eph. 4:24). After Augustine was converted, a woman he had formerly lived with called to him as he walked down the street, but he did not answer. She persisted and finally ran up to him and said, "Augustine, it is I." To which he replied, "I know, but it is no longer I."

REFLECTING ON THE TEXT

8) How much are you tempted to blame other people or circumstances for your own sin? What have you learned in this lesson about that tendency?

_____

_____

_____

_____

9) How would it change your life today (specifically and practically) if you could remember in each moment that the old you is dead and that God has given you a new nature (2 Cor. 5:17), one that loves God and hates sin?

_____

_____

_____

10) Pick one verse from this lesson that has proven especially meaningful to you. Write it out in the space below. Commit it to memory.

_____

_____

_____

_____

_____

_____

_____

_____

PERSONAL RESPONSE

Write out additional reflections, questions you may have, or a prayer.

_____

_____

_____

_____

_____

_____

_____

_____

_____

_____

_____

_____

_____

Additional Notes

3

BELIEF THAT BEHAVES
James 1:19–27

DRAWING NEAR

Rank the following behaviors in order of how reliable they are in pointing out true saving faith (1 = mark of a genuine believer; 10 = nothing to do with true faith).

_____ wears Christian T-shirts and jewelry

_____ has Christian bumper stickers on his or her car (and drives the speed limit!)

_____ gives regularly and sacrificially to the church

_____ participates in regular missions and outreach efforts

_____ sings in the choir (sometimes even solos)

_____ studies God's Word regularly and seeks to live it

_____ attends church faithfully

_____ has healthy, loving relationships with friends, family, coworkers, church members

_____ prays fervently for the lost

_____ owns all of Dr. MacArthur's writings and listens to all his sermons on tape

Why did you rank the items as you did? What do you think are the best indicators of true, saving faith?

_____

_____

_____

Are you a "doer" or a "watcher" when it comes to your spiritual growth and walk with God? Explain.

_____

_____

THE CONTEXT

In the passage before us, James presents another test of true believers. The first two tests centered around our response to trials and to temptation. The third test is our response to the truth revealed in the Word of God.

One of the most reliable evidences of genuine salvation is a hunger for the Word of God (see Ps. 42:1). Just as a newborn baby does not have to be taught to hunger for its mother's milk, the newborn child of God does not have to be taught to hunger for God's Word, his spiritual food and drink. When the true disciple hears God's Word, there is an affection for its truth and a desire in his heart to obey it. James focuses on a proper reception of Scripture as God's Word, and then on a proper reaction to it, reflected in an obedient life. As you study this passage, ask God to increase, or renew, your hunger for His Word and give you strength to do what it says.

KEYS TO THE TEXT

Doers: The substantive form of the Greek word *poiētē* ("doers") carries the characterization of the whole personality, all of a person's inner being—mind, soul, spirit, and emotions. It is one thing to have to fight for a few days or weeks in an armed conflict; it is something else to be a professional soldier, whose whole life is dedicated to warfare. It is one thing to make periodic repairs around the house; it is another to be a professional builder. Here James is speaking of Christian doers of the word, emphasizing what they are rather than just what they do. These are people whose very lives are dedicated not only to learning God's Word, but also to faithful and continual obedience to it. One commentator says that James has in mind "a person whose life is characterized by holy energy."

Hearers: The Greek word *akroatēs* ("hearers") was used of those who sat passively in an audience and listened to a singer or speaker. Today it could be used of those who audit a college class. Auditing requires attendance but does not require outside study or taking any tests. In other words, the auditor is not held accountable for what he hears. Tragically, most churches have many "auditors," members who take advantage of the privilege of hearing God's Word but have no desire for obeying it. When followed consistently, that attitude gives evidence that they are not Christians at all, but only pretenders. Such people—merely hearers and not also doers—think they belong to God, when, in reality, they do not. Proclaiming and interpreting God's Word are never ends in themselves but are means to an end, namely, the genuine acceptance of divine truth for what it is and the faithful application of it.

UNLEASHING THE TEXT

Read James 1:19–27, noting the key words and definitions next to the passage.

James 1:19–27 (NKJV)

19 So then, my beloved brethren, let every man be swift to hear, slow to speak, slow to wrath;

20 for the wrath of man does not produce the righteousness of God.

21 Therefore lay aside all filthiness and overflow of wickedness, and receive with meekness the implanted word, which is able to save your souls.

22 But be doers of the word, and not hearers only, deceiving yourselves.

23 For if anyone is a hearer of the word and not a doer, he is like a man observing his natural face in a mirror;

24 for he observes himself, goes away, and immediately forgets what kind of man he was.

25 But he who looks into the perfect law of liberty and continues in it, and is not a forgetful hearer but a doer of the work, this one will be blessed in what he does.

26 If anyone among you thinks he is religious, and does not bridle his tongue but deceives his own heart, this one's religion is useless.

swift to hear, slow to speak (v. 19)—Believers are to respond positively to Scripture and eagerly pursue every opportunity to know God's Word and will better. At the same time, they should be cautious about becoming a preacher or teacher themselves.

wrath (v. 20)—from the Greek word that describes a deep, internal resentment and rejection, in this context, of God's Word

lay aside (v. 21)—literally "having put off," as one would do with dirty clothes; the tense of this Greek verb stresses the importance of putting off sin prior to receiving God's Word

filthiness . . . wickedness (v. 21)—The first term was used of moral vice as well as dirty garments; sometimes it was even used of ear wax—here, of sin that would impede the believer's spiritual hearing. "Wickedness" refers to evil desire or intent.

deceiving (v. 22)—literally "reasoning beside or alongside" (as in "beside oneself"). This word was used in mathematics to refer to a miscalculation. Professing Christians who are content with only hearing the Word have made a serious spiritual miscalculation.

observing (v. 23)—look carefully and cautiously, as opposed to taking a casual glance

mirror (v. 23)—First-century mirrors were not glass but metallic, made of bronze, silver—or for the wealthy—gold. The metals were beaten flat and polished to a high gloss, and the image they reflected was adequate but not perfect.

forgets what kind of man he was (v. 24)—Unless professing Christians act promptly after they hear the Word, they will forget the changes and improvements that their reflection showed them they need to make.

perfect law (v. 25)—In both the Old and New Testaments, God's revealed, inerrant, sufficient, and comprehensive Word is called "law." The presence of His grace does not mean there is no moral law or code of conduct for believers to obey; rather, believers are enabled by the Spirit to keep this law.

liberty (v. 25)—genuine freedom from sin. As the Holy Spirit applies the principles of Scripture to believers' hearts, they are freed from sin's bondage and enabled to obey God.

religious (v. 26)—This refers to ceremonial public worship. James chose this term, instead of one referring to internal godliness, to emphasize the external trappings, rituals, routines, and forms that were not followed sincerely.

bridle his tongue (v. 26)—"Bridle" means "control," or as another translation renders it, "keep a tight rein." Purity of heart is often revealed by controlled and proper speech.

Pure and undefiled religion (v. 27)—James picks two synonymous adjectives to define the most spotless kind of religious faith—that which is measured by compassionate love.

27 *Pure and undefiled religion before God and the Father is this: to visit orphans and widows in their trouble, and to keep oneself unspotted from the world.*

orphans and widows (v. 27)—Those without parents or husbands were and are an especially needy segment of the church. Since they are usually unable to reciprocate in any way, caring for them clearly demonstrates true, sacrificial Christian love.

world (v. 27)—the evil world system

1) How will true believers behave (vv. 19–22)?

_____

_____

_____

_____

_____

2) In the arena of faith, how are the actions of "hearing" and "doing" different? How are they related?

_____

_____

_____

_____

3) What is the right response of a child of God to the Word of God? Why?

_____

_____

_____

_____

(Verses to consider: Ps.119:1, 10–11, 14; 2 Tim. 2:15; 1 John 2:24; 3:10)

4) What must we do to properly receive God's Word (v. 21)? How do we do this?

_____

_____

_____

_____

_____

_____

(Verses to consider: Rom. 13:12–14; Eph. 4:22–24; Col. 3:8; Heb. 12:1; 1 Pet. 2:1–2)

5) What examples does James give as behavior indicative of true faith? Why do you think he chooses these particular actions?

_____

_____

_____

_____

_____

(Verses to consider: Exod. 22:22–23; Deut. 14:28–29;
Ps. 68:5; Jer. 7:6–7; John 13:35; Acts 6:1–6; 1 Tim. 5:3)

GOING DEEPER

In a related passage, Jesus teaches on the importance of obedience and what that reveals. Read John 14:21–24.

21 *"He who has My commandments and keeps them, it is he who loves Me. And he who loves Me will be loved by My Father, and I will love him and manifest Myself to him."*

22 *Judas (not Iscariot) said to Him, "Lord, how is it that You will manifest Yourself to us, and not to the world?"*

23 *Jesus answered and said to him, "If anyone loves Me, he will keep My word; and My Father will love him, and We will come to him and make Our home with him.*

24 *He who does not love Me does not keep My words; and the word which you hear is not Mine but the Father's who sent Me."*

EXPLORING THE MEANING

6) How does Jesus relate love and obedience?

_____

_____

_____

_____

7) What does this teaching of Jesus add to your understanding of the relationship between true saving faith and obedience to the Word? What does obedience demonstrate?

_____

_____

_____

_____

8) Read Galatians 5:16–26. What resource does God give His children to ensure that they are able to live obediently?

_____

_____

_____

_____

(Verses to consider: John 8:31–36; 16:7–15)

TRUTH FOR TODAY

As important as the proper reception of the Word of God is, without obedience to its truths it is not only without benefit, but also becomes a further judgment against its readers. Obedience to the Word is the most basic spiritual requirement and is the common denominator for all true believers. The bottom line of true spiritual life is not a momentary feeling of compliance or commitment, but long-term obedience to Scripture.

Genuine believers receive Christ *and* continue in Him. They hear His Word *and* do it. They know His commandments, *and* they keep them. They do not claim to know God yet deny Him with their deeds. The validation of salvation is a life of obedience. It is the only possible proof that a person really knows Jesus

Christ. If one does not obey Christ as a pattern of life, then professing to know Him is an empty verbal exercise.

REFLECTING ON THE TEXT

9) Reflect on your life and habits. Do your actions show that you have received Christ *and* are following Him in obedience?

_____

_____

_____

_____

10) Why is humility necessary in hearing and obeying God's Word (James 1:21)?

_____

_____

_____

_____

11) When do you find it most difficult to approach Scripture with a humble heart and a teachable spirit?

_____

_____

_____

_____

12) Are you aware of any specific situations in your life in which you are not doing what you know God's Word calls you to do? Why the reluctance on your part to obey? Ask God to bring about His desired transformation in your life.

_____

_____

_____

_____

Personal Response

Write out additional reflections, questions you may have, or a prayer.

4

FAVORITISM IN THE CHURCH?
James 2:1–13

DRAWING NEAR

It has been said that the most segregated time of the week in this culture is the Sunday morning worship hour. In what ways, if any, have you seen this to be true in your church (e.g., financial, racial, social, theological, etc.)?

_____

_____

_____

_____

Have you experienced negative prejudicial treatment from someone? Explain the situation. How did it feel?

_____

_____

_____

_____

Have you experienced positive preferential treatment from someone? Explain the situation. How did it feel?

_____

_____

_____

_____

THE CONTEXT

An attribute of God that is not often thought about is His impartiality. Yet this is a recurring theme throughout Scripture. God is absolutely impartial in His dealings with people. And in that way, as with other attributes, He is unlike us. Human beings (and that includes Christians) are not naturally inclined to be impartial. We tend to put people in pigeonholes, in predetermined categories, ranking them by their looks, their clothes, their race or ethnicity, their social status, their personality, their intelligence, their wealth and power, by the kind of car they drive, and by the type of house and neighborhood they live in. But those things are non-issues with God and are of no significance to Him. God looks at the heart and loves all people equally. He wants us to do the same.

James's practical epistle deals more with day-to-day issues than with theology and doctrine. In this passage, he stresses that showing partiality, or not showing it, is another kind of test of true and living faith. He focuses mostly on partiality in regard to social and economic status. Doubtless, these issues were special problems in the early church and were obviously problems with some of the Jewish believers "scattered abroad" (1:1). James presents five features of genuine, Godlike impartiality: the principle (v. 1), the example (vv. 2–4), the inconsistency (vv. 5–7), the violation (vv. 8–11), and the appeal (vv. 12–13).

KEYS TO THE TEXT

Partiality: This refers to an attitude of personal favoritism. Translated from the single Greek word *prosōpolēmpsia,* it has the literal meaning of lifting up someone's face, with the idea of judging by appearance and, on that basis, giving special favor and respect. This word originally referred to raising someone's face or elevating the person, but it came to refer to exalting someone strictly on a superficial, external basis—such as appearance, race, wealth, rank, or social status, without consideration of a person's true merits, abilities, or character. It is both interesting and significant that this word, along with the related noun *prosōpolēmptēs* (see Acts 10:34, "partiality") and the verb *prosōpolēmpteō* (see 2:9, "show partiality") are found only in Christian writings. Perhaps that is because favoritism was such an accepted part of most ancient societies that it was assumed and not even identified, as it still is in many cultures today.

UNLEASHING THE TEXT

Read James 2:1–13, noting the key words and definitions next to the passage.

the faith (v. 1)—This refers not to the act of believing, but to the entire Christian faith (see Jude 3), which has as its central focus Jesus Christ.

James 2:1–13 (NKJV)

1 *My brethren, do not hold the faith of our Lord Jesus Christ, the Lord of glory, with partiality.*

the Lord of glory (v. 1)—Christ is the One who reveals the glory of God. In His incarnation, He showed only impartiality (see Matt. 22:16)—for example, consider the variety of people included in His genealogy, His choice of the humble village of Nazareth as His residence for thirty years, and His willingness to minister in Galilee and Samaria, both regions held in contempt by Israel's leaders.

assembly (v. 2)—literally "a gathering together" or "synagogue." Since James was writing early in the church's history to Jewish believers (1:1), he used both this general word and the normal Greek word for "church" (5:14) to describe the church's corporate meetings during that period of transition.

2 *For if there should come into your assembly a man with gold rings, in fine apparel, and there should also come in a poor man in filthy clothes,*

3 *and you pay attention to the one wearing the fine clothes and say to him, "You sit here in a good place," and say to the poor man, "You stand there," or, "Sit here at my footstool,"*

4 *have you not shown partiality among yourselves, and become judges with evil thoughts?*

5 *Listen, my beloved brethren: Has God not chosen the poor of this world to be rich in faith and heirs of the kingdom which He promised to those who love Him?*

6 *But you have dishonored the poor man. Do not the rich oppress you and drag you into the courts?*

7 *Do they not blaspheme that noble name by which you are called?*

8 *If you really fulfill the royal law according to the Scripture, "You shall love your neighbor as yourself," you do well;*

gold rings (v. 2)—While Jews commonly wore rings, few could afford gold ones; however, there are some reports that in the ancient world the most ostentatious people wore rings on every finger but the middle one to show off their economic status (some ancient sources indicate that there were even ring rental businesses).

fine apparel (v. 2)—This word refers to bright, shining garments and is used of the gorgeous garment Herod's soldiers put on Jesus to mock Him, and of the apparel of an angel. It can also refer to bright, flashy color and to brilliant, glittering, sparkling ornamentation. James is not condemning this unbeliever for his distracting dress, but rather the church's flattering reaction to it.

a poor man (v. 2)—Although there were people of means in the early church (1 Tim. 6:17–19), it consisted mostly of common, poor people (see James 5; Acts 2:45). Throughout Scripture, the poor are objects of God's special concern (1:27).

sit . . . in a good place (v. 3)—a more comfortable, prominent place of honor. The synagogues and assembly halls of the first century sometimes had benches around the outside wall and a couple of benches in front; but most of the congregation either sat cross-legged on the floor or stood. There were a limited number of good seats; and they were the ones the Pharisees always wanted (Mark 12:38–39).

shown partiality (v. 4)—the true nature of the sin in this passage, not the lavish apparel or rings of the rich man or that he was given a good seat

judges with evil thoughts (v. 4)—This is better translated "judges with vicious intentions." James feared that his readers would behave just like the sinful world by catering to the rich and prominent while shunning the poor and common.

the kingdom (v. 5)—Here James intends the kingdom in its present sense of the sphere of salvation—those over whom Christ rules—as well as its future millennial and eternal glory.

oppress (v. 6)—literally "to tyrannize"

drag you into the courts (v. 6)—a reference to civil court

blaspheme that noble name (v. 7)—probably a reference to religious courts. Wealthy Jewish opponents of Christ were harassing these poor Christians.

royal law (v. 8)—This is better translated "sovereign law"; the idea is that this law is supreme or binding.

love your neighbor as yourself (v. 8)—This sovereign law, when combined with the command to love God, summarizes all the Law and the Prophets. James is not advocating some kind of emotional affection for one's self, for self-love is clearly a sin; rather, the command is to pursue meeting the physical health and spiritual well-being of one's neighbors (all within the sphere of our influence; Luke 10:30–37) with the same intensity and concern as one does naturally for oneself (see Phil. 2:3–4).

if (v. 9)—Better translated as "since," the Greek construction of this conditional statement indicates that this practice was in fact happening among James's readers.

show partiality (v. 9)—The form of this Greek verb indicates that their behavior was not an occasional slip but a continual practice.

convicted by the law (v. 9)—specifically by the commands in Deuteronomy 1:17 and 16:19

transgressors (v. 9)—This refers to one who goes beyond the law of God. Respect of persons makes one a violator of God's law.

9 but if you show partiality, you commit sin, and are convicted by the law as transgressors.

10 For whoever shall keep the whole law, and yet stumble in one point, he is guilty of all.

11 For He who said, "Do not commit adultery," also said, "Do not murder." Now if you do not commit adultery, but you do murder, you have become a transgressor of the law.

12 So speak and so do as those who will be judged by the law of liberty.

13 For judgment is without mercy to the one who has shown no mercy. Mercy triumphs over judgment.

whole law . . . one point (v. 10)—The law of God is not a series of detached injunctions but a basic unity that requires perfect love of Him and our neighbors. Although all sins are not equally damaging or heinous, they all shatter that unity and render men transgressors, much like hitting a window with a hammer at only one point will shatter and destroy the whole window.

guilty of all (v. 10)—not in the sense of having violated every command, but in the sense of having violated the law's unity. One transgression makes fulfilling the law's most basic commands—to love God perfectly and to love one's neighbor as oneself—impossible.

the one who has shown no mercy (v. 13)—The person who shows no mercy and compassion for people in need demonstrates that he has never responded to the great mercy of God, and as an unredeemed person will receive only strict, unrelieved judgment in eternal hell (see Matt. 5:7).

Mercy triumphs over judgment (v. 13)—The person whose life is characterized by mercy is ready for the day of judgment and he will escape all the charges that strict justice might bring against him. By showing mercy to others, he gives proof of having received God's mercy.

1) According to James, why is showing partiality incompatible with faith?

_____

_____

_____

_____

_____

_____

(Verses to consider: Lev. 19:15; Deut. 10:17; 15:7–10; 2 Chron. 19:7; Job 34:19; Prov. 24:23; 28:21; Acts 10:34–35; Rom. 2:11; Eph. 6:9; 1 Pet. 1:17)

2) Was the early church primarily composed of rich people or poor? On what do you base your answer?

_____

_____

_____

_____

_____

3) What reaction did the poor often get when they visited a Christian assembly? What did James remind his readers about the poor?

_____

_____

_____

_____

_____

(Verses to consider: Lev. 25:35–37; Ps. 41:1; 72:4, 12; 113:7; Prov. 17:5; 21:13; 28:27; 29:7; 31:9; Isa. 3:14–15; 10:1–2; 25:4; Gal. 2:10)

4) How does James use the law to explain the problem of partiality (vv. 8–10)?

_____

_____

_____

_____

5) What did James mean by using the seemingly paradoxical phrase of "law of liberty"?

_____

_____

_____

_____

_____

GOING DEEPER

The royal law of love that James mentioned was part of Jesus' teaching. Read Matthew 22:34–40.

> 34 But when the Pharisees heard that He [Jesus] had silenced the Sadducees, they gathered together.
> 35 Then one of them, a lawyer, asked Him a question, testing Him, and saying,
> 36 "Teacher, which is the great commandment in the law?"
> 37 Jesus said to him, 'You shall love the LORD your God with all your heart, with all your soul, and with all your mind.'
> 38 This is the first and great commandment.
> 39 And the second is like it: 'You shall love your neighbor as yourself.'
> 40 On these two commandments hang all the Law and the Prophets."

EXPLORING THE MEANING

6) How can obeying these great commands eliminate the sin of partiality and favoritism among people of faith?

_____

_____

_____

_____

_____

_____

(Verses to consider: Deut. 6:4–5; Rom. 13:8–10)

7) Read 2 Timothy 3:1–5. How do these verses shatter the common myth that the command "love your neighbor as yourself" is actually a call for people to love themselves?

_____

_____

_____

_____

_____

8) Read Philippians 2:3–4. What does this passage (and its context) say about our attitudes and relating to others?

_____

_____

_____

_____

_____

Truth for Today

There will be no poor in heaven in any sense, no second-class citizens. Everyone will be rich in the things that matter eternally. Every believer will receive the same eternal life, the same heavenly citizenship in the kingdom of God, and the same perfect righteousness of Christ imputed to them by the Father. Every one of His children will live in His house and bask alike in His presence and love (John 14:1–3).

Reflecting on the Text

9) Numerous passages in Scripture call on believers to show compassion to the poor. Identify two or three concrete ways you can begin to obey this command this week.

_____

_____

_____

_____

_____

10) What is at the root of favoritism, the cause of showing partiality?

_____

_____

_____

_____

11) What are some ways of "labeling" others that you need to refrain from using immediately?

_____

_____

_____

_____

12) In what ways do you struggle with showing preferential treatment to some and prejudice against others? What are two specific ways you can begin loving people as God does this week in your home? In the workplace? At your church?

_____

_____

_____

_____

Personal Response

Write out additional reflections, questions you may have, or a prayer.

_____

_____

_____

_____

_____

_____

_____

_____

_____

_____

_____

_____

5

DEAD FAITH
James 2:14–20

DRAWING NEAR

How do you define *faith*?

_____

_____

_____

_____

How would you explain to a child why we do "good works"?

_____

_____

_____

_____

_____

THE CONTEXT

James continues his series of tests by which his readers can evaluate whether their faith is living or dead. And he clearly says that a faith that is not acted out is really no faith at all. He's not saying that a person is saved by works (he has already clearly asserted in 1:17–18 that salvation is a gracious gift from God). He is saying that there is a kind of *apparent* faith that is dead and does not save (vv. 14, 17, 20, 24, 26). It is possible James was writing to Jewish Christians who had embraced the mistaken notion that since righteous works and obedience to God's law were not efficacious for salvation, they were not necessary at all. Thus they reduced "faith" to a mere mental assent to the facts about Christ.

The truth that James emphasizes in this text is that *what we do reveals who we are.* He is not speaking simply of beliefs and intentions in general, but of the foundational belief of saving faith. The genuineness of one's profession of faith in Jesus Christ as Savior and Lord is evidenced more by what a person does than by what he claims. As you study the passage, ask God to give you insight into the important relationship between faith and works, and to help you have a living faith.

Keys to the Text

Faith: James does not mention a particular kind of faith, but the context indicates that it refers to acknowledging the basic truths of the gospel. A person making such a claim would believe in such things as the existence of God, Scripture as the Word of God, and, presumably, in the messiahship of Christ and in His atoning death, resurrection, and ascension. In any case, the theological orthodoxy of such a person's faith is not in question; the issue is that he has no works. The verb form in that phrase describes someone who continually lacks evidence to support the claim of faith he routinely makes.

Unleashing the Text

Read James 2:14–20, noting the key words and definitions next to the passage.

if someone says (v. 14)—This important phrase governs the interpretation of the entire passage. James does not say that this person actually has faith, but that he claims to have it.

faith (v. 14)—This is best understood in a broad sense, speaking of any degree of acceptance of the truths of the gospel.

does not have (v. 14)—Again, the verb's form describes someone who continually lacks any external evidence of the faith he routinely claims.

works (v. 14)—This refers to all righteous behavior that conforms to God's revealed Word, but specifically, in the context, to acts of compassion (v. 15).

James 2:14–20 (NKJV)

14 *What does it profit, my brethren, if someone says he has faith but does not have works? Can faith save him?*

15 *If a brother or sister is naked and destitute of daily food,*

16 *and one of you says to them, "Depart in peace, be warmed and filled," but you do not give them the things which are needed for the body, what does it profit?*

17 *Thus also faith by itself, if it does not have works, is dead.*

18 *But someone will say, "You have faith, and I have works." Show me your faith without your works, and I will show you my faith by my works.*

Can faith save him? (v. 14)—better translated, "Can that kind of faith save?" James is not disputing the importance of faith; rather, he is opposing the notion that saving faith can be a mere intellectual exercise void of a commitment to active obedience. The grammatical form of the question demands a negative answer.

faith by itself . . . is dead (v. 17)—Just as professed compassion without action is phony, the kind of faith that is without works is mere empty profession, not genuine saving faith.

someone (v. 18)—Interpreters disagree on (1) whether "someone" is James's humble way of referring to himself or whether it refers to one of James's antagonists who objected to his teaching; and (2) how much of the following passage should be attributed to this antagonist as opposed to James himself. Regardless, James's main point is the same: The only possible evidence of true faith is works.

You believe that there is one God. (v. 19)—a clear reference to the passage most familiar to his Jewish readers—the shema (Deut. 6:4–5), the most basic doctrine of the Old Testament

19 *You believe that there is one God. You do well. Even the demons believe—and tremble!*

20 *But do you want to know, O foolish man, that faith without works is dead?*

demons believe (v. 18)—Even fallen angels affirm the oneness of God and tremble at its implications. Demons are essentially orthodox in their doctrine, but orthodox doctrine by itself is no proof of saving faith. They know the truth about God, Christ, and the Spirit, but hate it and them.

foolish (v. 20)—literally "empty, defective." The objector's claim of belief is fraudulent, and his faith is a sham.

faith without works is dead (v. 20)—literally "the faith without the works." James is not contrasting two methods of salvation (faith versus works); instead, he contrasts two kinds of faith: living faith that saves and dead faith that does not.

1) What two examples does James cite to show the futility of faith without works (vv. 15–16, 19)? How are these good examples of dead faith?

_____

_____

_____

_____

2) Do you think James proves his point? Why do you think so?

_____

_____

_____

_____

_____

3) Is James suggesting that helping the poor and hungry is a prerequisite to salvation? How do you know?

_____

_____

_____

_____

_____

4) What did James mean when he said that the "demons believe"? How does this emphasize the difference between dead faith and genuine saving faith?

_____

_____

_____

_____

_____

_____

(Verses to consider: Matt. 8:29; Mark 5:7; Luke 4:41; Acts 19:15)

GOING DEEPER

Jesus told a parable that also illustrates how true faith reveals itself through doing good to others. Read Matthew 25:31–46.

31 *When the Son of Man comes in His glory, and all the holy angels with Him, then He will sit on the throne of His glory.*

32 *All the nations will be gathered before Him, and He will separate them one from another, as a shepherd divides his sheep from the goats.*

33 *And He will set the sheep on His right hand, but the goats on the left.*

34 *Then the King will say to those on His right hand, "Come, you blessed of My Father, inherit the kingdom prepared for you from the foundation of the world:*

35 *for I was hungry and you gave Me food; I was thirsty and you gave Me drink; I was a stranger and you took Me in;*

36 *I was naked and you clothed Me; I was sick and you visited Me; I was in prison and you came to Me."*

37 *Then the righteous will answer Him, saying, "Lord, when did we see You hungry and feed You, or thirsty and give You drink?*

38 *When did we see You a stranger and take You in, or naked and clothe You?*

39 *Or when did we see You sick, or in prison, and come to You?"*

40 *And the King will answer and say to them, "Assuredly, I say to you, inasmuch as you did it to one of the least of these My brethren, you did it to Me."*

41 *"Then He will also say to those on the left hand, 'Depart from Me, you cursed, into the everlasting fire prepared for the devil and his angels:*

42 *for I was hungry and you gave Me no food; I was thirsty and you gave Me no drink;*

43 *I was a stranger and you did not take Me in, naked and you did not clothe Me, sick and in prison and you did not visit Me."*

44 *Then they also will answer Him, saying, "Lord, when did we see You hungry or thirsty or a stranger or naked or sick or in prison, and did not minister to You?"*

45 *Then He will answer them, saying, "Assuredly, I say to you, inasmuch as you did not do it to one of the least of these, you did not do it to Me."*

46 *And these will go away into everlasting punishment, but the righteous into eternal life.*

EXPLORING THE MEANING

5) What does this parable reveal about the relationship between faith and works? How is the King able to tell which are his true subjects?

_____

_____

_____

_____

6) Read Ephesians 2:8–10. What more do you learn about the relationship between salvation and works?

_____

_____

_____

_____

7) Read Luke 19:1–10. What does this incident reveal about the transforming nature of saving faith?

_____

_____

_____

_____

(Verses to consider: Acts 19:18–19; 1 Thess. 1:9)

TRUTH FOR TODAY

It cannot be stressed too often that no one can be saved by works. Salvation is entirely "by grace . . . through faith, and that not of yourselves; it is the gift of God, not of works, lest anyone should boast" (Eph. 2:8–9). If works could have any part in salvation, it would no longer be by God's grace. But neither can it be stressed too often that, as James declares in the present passage, "faith by itself, if it does not have works, is dead" (2:17). Genuine, transforming faith not only should, but *will*, produce genuine good works, notably repentance and obedient submission to Christ's lordship. This is the expression of the new nature, created in the new birth (2 Cor. 5:17). It will not be perfect obedience and repentance, but good works will be present. We might say that it costs us *nothing* to become a Christian but *everything* to live fully as one.

REFLECTING ON THE TEXT

8) Martin Luther wrote, "If works and love do not blossom forth, it is not genuine faith, the gospel has not yet gained a foothold, and Christ is not yet rightly known." Stop and reflect on this. Has the gospel gained a foothold in your life? How can you blossom forth in love and good works this week?

_____

_____

_____

_____

_____

9) What have you learned about the dangers of only doing good works? Of only having a head-knowledge faith?

_____

_____

_____

_____

_____

_____

10) Someone has asked, "If you were tried in a court of law for being a Christian, would there be enough evidence to convict you?" How would you answer this? What undeniable proof of God's saving and sanctifying work do you see in your life?

_____

_____

_____

_____

_____

_____

Personal Response

Write out additional reflections, questions you may have, or a prayer.

_____

_____

_____

_____

_____

_____

_____

_____

_____

_____

_____

_____

_____

_____

_____

Additional Notes

6

FAITH THAT PASSES THE TEST
James 2:21–26

DRAWING NEAR

What is the greatest step of faith you have ever seen someone take?

_____

_____

_____

_____

Do you think some Christians have a greater capacity for faith than others? If so, why?

_____

_____

_____

_____

When in your life have you taken a great risk and followed what you believed to be God's will, even though some friends and family felt your decision to be foolish? How did you feel in the midst of that time? What finally happened?

_____

_____

_____

_____

THE CONTEXT

James has contrasted living faith with dead faith, saving faith with non-saving faith, productive faith with unproductive faith, godly faith with a kind of faith that is exercised even by demons. Now he continues his argument by giving real-life illustrations of living faith: Abraham and Rahab. They were justified not by their words of faith, or worship ritual, or any other religious activity. In both cases their faith was demonstrated by action, by putting everything that was dear to them on the line for the Lord and entrusting it to Him without qualification or reservation. They were supremely committed to the Lord, whatever the cost.

It is in the vortex of the great plans, decisions, and crossroads of life—where ambitions, hopes, dreams, destinies, and life itself are at stake—that true faith unfailingly reveals itself. Long before Jesus' crucifixion, Abraham and Rahab were willing to take up their crosses, as it were, and follow Him (Mark 8:34). They hated their life in this world in order to keep it in the world to come (John 12:25). Abraham and Rahab stand for all time as examples of those whose living faith passed the test.

KEYS TO THE TEXT

Abraham: Abraham was the Old Testament patriarch of the Hebrew nation. In Genesis 22 God told Abraham to take "your son . . . and offer him." These startling commands activated a special testing ordeal for Abraham, i.e., to sacrifice his "only son" Isaac. This sacrifice meant killing on the altar the son he had waited so long for and had now watched grow for perhaps twenty years. It meant not only cutting off his son's life, but also cutting off the channel through which God had promised to fulfill the Abrahamic Covenant that would make Abraham the father of a great nation. Though God's command may not have made sense, Abraham obeyed in faith, and God stopped him before the act. It was that faith that God honored. Although James's primary audience was Jewish, the context suggests that his reference to Abraham our father is not racial. He seems rather to write of Abraham in the same spiritual sense that Paul does in several places, that "those who are of faith . . . are sons of Abraham" (Gal. 3:7). Abraham is the model of saving faith for both Jew and Gentile, a man whose faith was living and acceptable to God.

UNLEASHING THE TEXT

Read James 2:21–26, noting the key words and definitions next to the passage.

justified by works (v. 21)—This does not contradict Paul's clear teaching that Abraham was justified before God by grace alone through faith alone. For several

James 2:21–26 (NKJV)

21 *Was not Abraham our father justified by works when he offered Isaac his son on the altar?*

reasons, James cannot mean that Abraham was constituted righteous before God because of his own good works: (1) James already stressed that salvation is a gracious gift (1:17–18); (2) in the middle of this disputed passage (v. 23), James quoted Genesis 15:6, which forcefully claims that God credited righteousness to Abraham solely on the basis of his faith; and (3) the work that James said justified Abraham was his offering up of Isaac, an event that occurred many years after he first exercised faith and was declared righteous before God. Instead, Abraham's offering of Isaac demonstrated the genuineness of his faith and the reality of his justification before God. James is emphasizing the vindication before others of a man's claim to salvation. His teaching perfectly complements Paul's writings; salvation is determined by faith alone (Eph. 2:8–9) and demonstrated by faithfulness to obey God's will alone (Eph. 2:10).

22 *Do you see that faith was working together with his works, and by works faith was made perfect?*

23 *And the Scripture was fulfilled which says, "Abraham believed God, and it was accounted to him for righteousness." And he was called the friend of God.*

24 *You see then that a man is justified by works, and not by faith only.*

25 *Likewise, was not Rahab the harlot also justified by works when she received the messengers and sent them out another way?*

26 *For as the body without the spirit is dead, so faith without works is dead also.*

was made perfect (v. 22)—This refers to bringing something to its end, or to its fullness. Just as a fruit tree has not arrived at its goal until it bears fruit, faith has not reached its end until it demonstrates itself in a righteous life.

the Scripture . . . says (v. 23)—quoted from Genesis 15:6

friend of God (v. 23)—so called because of his obedience

Rahab the harlot (v. 25)—The Old Testament records the content of her faith, which was the basis of her justification before God; she demonstrated the reality of her saving faith when, at great personal risk she protected the messengers of God. James did not intend, however, for those words to be a commendation of her occupation or her lying.

justified by works (*v.* 25)—The Greek verb *dikaioo* ("justified") has two general meanings. The first pertains to acquittal, that is, to declaring and treating a person as righteous; that is its meaning in relationship to salvation and is the sense in which Paul almost always uses the term. The second meaning of *dikaioo* pertains to vindication, or proof of righteousness; it is used in that sense a number of times in the New Testament, in relation to God as well as men. It is this second meaning that is in view in this passage. James says that Abraham, whose very faith itself was a gift of God (Eph. 2:8), was nevertheless justified by works. That seeming contradiction, which has frustrated and confused believers throughout the history of the church, is clarified by understanding that justification by faith pertains to a person's standing before God, whereas the justification by works that James speaks of in this verse pertains to a person's standing before other men.

1) What three illustrations does James give to continue illustrating his point that faith without works is dead?

_____

_____

_____

_____

_____

_____

(Verses to consider: Gen. 22:1–19; Josh. 2:1–21, 6:22–23)

2) Paul taught that we are justified by faith alone. James says that Abraham and Rahab were justified by works. When you look at the whole of what James has been saying about faith and works, you can see how the paradox resolves itself. How would you explain this seeming contradiction to someone else?

_____

_____

_____

_____

_____

_____

(Verses to consider: John 8:56; 14:6; Acts 4:12; Eph. 2:8–9; Heb. 5:9; 11:8–10, 13–16, 31)

3) Why is it significant that Abraham was called "the friend of God"? What does this mean?

_____

_____

_____

_____

_____

_____

(Verses to consider: 2 Chron. 20:7; Isa. 41:8; John 15:14–15)

4) How would you answer the person who argued from James 2:21 that our works (or behavior) do play an important role in our salvation?

_____

_____

_____

_____

_____

_____

(Verses to consider: Rom. 3:20; Gal. 3:6–11)

GOING DEEPER

For more insight about Abraham's faith, read Romans 4:1–25.

1 *What then shall we say that Abraham our father has found according to the flesh?*

2 *For if Abraham was justified by works, he has something to boast about, but not before God.*

3 *For what does the Scripture say? "Abraham believed God, and it was accounted to him for righteousness."*

4 *Now to him who works, the wages are not counted as grace but as debt.*

5 *But to him who does not work but believes on Him who justifies the ungodly, his faith is accounted for righteousness,*

6 *just as David also describes the blessedness of the man to whom God imputes righteousness apart from works:*

7 *"Blessed are those whose lawless deeds are forgiven, and whose sins are covered;*

8 *Blessed is the man to whom the LORD shall not impute sin."*

9 *Does this blessedness then come upon the circumcised only, or upon the uncircumcised also? For we say that faith was accounted to Abraham for righteousness.*

10 *How then was it accounted? While he was circumcised, or uncircumcised? Not while circumcised, but while uncircumcised.*

11 *And he received the sign of circumcision, a seal of the righteousness of the faith which he had while still uncircumcised, that he might be the father of all those who believe, though they are uncircumcised, that righteousness might be imputed to them also,*

12 *and the father of circumcision to those who not only are of the circumcision, but who also walk in the steps of the faith which our father Abraham had while still uncircumcised.*

13 *For the promise that he would be the heir of the world was not to Abraham or to his seed through the law, but through the righteousness of faith.*

14 *For if those who are of the law are heirs, faith is made void and the promise made of no effect,*

15 *because the law brings about wrath; for where there is no law there is no transgression.*

16 *Therefore it is of faith that it might be according to grace, so that the promise might be sure to all the seed, not only to those who are of the law, but also to those who are of the faith of Abraham, who is the father of us all*

17 *(as it is written, "I have made you a father of many nations") in the presence of Him whom he believed—God, who gives life to the dead and calls those things which do not exist as though they did;*

18 *who, contrary to hope, in hope believed, so that he became the father of many nations, according to what was spoken, "So shall your descendants be."*

19 *And not being weak in faith, he did not consider his own body, already dead (since he was about a hundred years old), and the deadness of Sarah's womb.*

20 *He did not waver at the promise of God through unbelief, but was strengthened in faith, giving glory to God,*

21 *and being fully convinced that what He had promised He was also able to perform.*

22 *And therefore "it was accounted to him for righteousness."*

23 *Now it was not written for his sake alone that it was imputed to him,*

24 *but also for us. It shall be imputed to us who believe in Him who raised up Jesus our Lord from the dead,*

25 *who was delivered up because of our offenses, and was raised because of our justification.*

EXPLORING THE MEANING

5) What insights does this passage contribute to your understanding of the relationship between faith and works?

_____

_____

_____

_____

_____

6) What do you learn about faith from Abraham's life?

_____

_____

_____

_____

(Verses to consider: Heb. 11:8–19)

7) Look at the description of faith in Romans 4:20–22. Have you experienced faith like this? How does this expand your own understanding of living faith?

_____

_____

_____

_____

_____

_____

8) Read 2 Corinthians 13:5. In light of the reality of dead faith that often masquerades as saving faith, what should professing Christians do?

_____

_____

_____

_____

_____

TRUTH FOR TODAY

Abraham was not a perfect man, either in his faith or in his works. After many years had passed without Sarah's having the promised heir, he took matters into his own hands, having a son, Ishmael, by Hagar, his wife's maid. His wavering trust in the Lord led him to commit adultery. In those and other instances, such as when he lied twice about Sarah being his sister (Gen. 12:19; 20:2), his works obviously did not justify him before men.

But James's point is that, in the overall pattern of his life, Abraham faithfully vindicated his saving faith through his many good works, above all else by offering Isaac as a sacrifice. When a man is justified before God, he will always prove that justification before other men. A man who has been declared and made righteous will live righteously. Imputed righteousness will manifest practical righteousness. In the words of John Calvin, "Faith alone justifies; but the faith that justifies is never alone."

Reflecting on the Text

9) In the overall pattern of your life, do your actions vindicate that you do, in fact, possess saving faith? Explain your answer.

_____

_____

_____

_____

10) Why should Rahab's inclusion in this passage be a great encouragement to modern-day Christians?

_____

_____

_____

_____

11) What are some simple but concrete "faith steps" you could take today to force yourself out of your "comfort zone" and into a position where you have no choice but to rely on God?

_____

_____

_____

_____

Personal Response

Write out additional reflections, questions you may have, or a prayer.

_____

_____

_____

_____

_____

_____

7

TAMING THE TONGUE
James 3:1–12

DRAWING NEAR

What kind of speech generally rolls off your tongue and out of your mouth? Think about your speech over the last week and give yourself a "thumbs up" (i.e., I'm innocent!) or a "thumbs down" (i.e., I'm guilty!) in the following categories:

	Thumbs Up!	**Thumbs Down!**
Bragging/boasting		
Lying		
Flattering		
Slandering		
Gossiping		
Verbally abusing others		
Cursing		
Making off-color remarks		
Talking behind another's back		
Passing on rumors		
Shading the truth		
Arguing		
Yelling		
Being sarcastic or cutting		
Teaching questionable "truths"		

Which of these "sins of the tongue" seem to trip you up most often? Why?

_____

_____

_____

_____

THE CONTEXT

The tongue is you in a unique way. It is a tattletale that tells on the heart and discloses the real person. Not only that, but misuse of the tongue is perhaps the easiest way to sin. There are some sins that an individual may not be able to commit simply because he does not have the opportunity. But there are no limits to what one can say, no built-in restraints or boundaries. In Scripture, the tongue is variously described as wicked, deceitful, perverse, filthy, corrupt, flattering, slanderous, gossiping, blasphemous, foolish, boasting, complaining, cursing, contentious, sensual, and vile. And that list is not exhaustive. No wonder God put the tongue in a cage behind the teeth, walled in by the mouth!

Not surprisingly, the tongue is of great concern to James, being mentioned in every chapter of his letter (see 1:19, 26; 2:12; 3:5, 6, 8; 4:11; 5:12). In 3:1–12 he uses the tongue as still another test of living faith, because the genuineness of a person's faith will inevitably be demonstrated by his speech. James personifies the tongue and the mouth as representatives of the depravity and wretchedness of the inner person. The tongue only produces what it is told to produce by the heart, where sin originates (see 1:14–15).

In summary, James teaches that true believers will possess a sanctified tongue, yet they must maintain a sanctified tongue. He gives three compelling reasons for controlling the tongue: its potential to condemn; its power to control; and its propensity to corrupt.

KEYS TO THE TEXT

The Tongue: In this passage, James used the common Jewish literary device of attributing blame to a specific bodily member (see Rom. 3:15; 2 Pet. 2:14). He personified the tongue as being representative of human depravity and wretchedness. In this way, he echoed the scriptural truth that the mouth is a focal point and vivid indicator of man's fallenness and sinful heart condition (Matt. 15:11, 16–19; Rom. 3:13–14). He called the tongue an "unruly evil," from the Greek word *akatastatos,* the same word rendered "unstable" in 1:8. In this context, the meaning suggests the idea of a wild animal fighting fiercely against the restraints of captivity. This evil chafes at confinement, always seeking a way to escape and to spread its deadly poison. Its "venom" is more deadly than a snake's because it can destroy morally, socially, economically, and spiritually.

UNLEASHING THE TEXT

Read James 3:1–12, noting the key words and definitions next to the passage.

James 3:1–12 (NKJV)

1 *My brethren, let not many of you become teachers, knowing that we shall receive a stricter judgment.*

2 *For we all stumble in many things. If anyone does not stumble in word, he is a perfect man, able also to bridle the whole body.*

3 *Indeed, we put bits in horses' mouths that they may obey us, and we turn their whole body.*

4 *Look also at ships: although they are so large and are driven by fierce winds, they are turned by a very small rudder wherever the pilot desires.*

5 *Even so the tongue is a little member and boasts great things. See how great a forest a little fire kindles!*

6 *And the tongue is a fire, a world of iniquity. The tongue is so set among our members that it defiles the whole body, and sets on fire the course of nature; and it is set on fire by hell.*

7 *For every kind of beast and bird, of reptile and creature of the sea, is tamed and has been tamed by mankind.*

8 *But no man can tame the tongue. It is an unruly evil, full of deadly poison.*

9 *With it we bless our God and Father, and with it we curse men, who have been made in the similitude of God.*

teachers (v. 1)—This word is translated "master" in the Gospels and refers to a person who functions in an official teaching or preaching capacity

stricter judgment (v. 1)—The word translated "judgment" usually expresses a negative verdict in the New Testament, and here refers to a future judgment: (1) for the unbelieving false teacher, at the Second Coming (Jude 14–15); and (2) for the believer, when he is rewarded before Christ (1 Cor. 4:3–5). This is not meant to discourage true teachers, but to warn the prospective teacher of the role's seriousness.

stumble (v. 2)—This refers to sinning, or offending God's Person; the form of the Greek verb emphasizes that everyone continually fails to do what is right.

perfect man (v. 2)—"Perfect" may refer to true perfection, in which case James is saying that, hypothetically, if a human being were able to perfectly control his tongue, he would be a perfect man. Of course, no one is actually immune from sinning with his tongue; so more likely, "perfect" is describing those who are spiritually mature and thus able to control their tongues.

tongue is a fire (v. 6)—Like fire, the tongue's sinful words can spread destruction rapidly, or as its accompanying smoke, those words can permeate and ruin everything around it.

defiles (v. 6)—This means "to pollute or contaminate" (see Mark 7:20; Jude 23).

the course of nature (v. 6)—Better translated "the circle of life," this underscores that the tongue's evil can extend beyond the individual to affect everything in his sphere of influence.

hell (v. 6)—a translation of the Greek word *gehenna* (or "valley of Hinnom"). In Christ's time this valley that lay southwest of Jerusalem's walls served as the city dump and was known for its constantly burning fire. Jesus used that place to symbolize the eternal place of punishment and torment. To James, "hell" conjures up not just the place but the satanic host that will some day inherit it—they use the tongue as a tool for evil.

no man can tame the tongue (v. 8)—Only God, by His power, can do this (see Acts 2:1–11).

bless . . . curse (v. 9)—It was traditional for Jews to add "blessed be He" to a mention of God's name; however, the tongue also wishes evil on people made in God's image. This points out the hypocritical inconsistency of the tongue's activities.

made in the similitude of God (v. 9)—Man was made in God's image.

53

spring . . . fig tree . . . salt water (vv. 11–12)—Three illustrations from nature demonstrate
the sinfulness of cursing. The
genuine believer will not contradict his profession of faith by
the regular use of unwholesome
words.

10 Out of the same mouth proceed blessing and cursing.
My brethren, these things ought not to be so.

11 Does a spring send forth fresh water and bitter from
the same opening?

12 Can a fig tree, my brethren, bear olives, or a
grapevine bear figs? Thus no spring yields both salt
water and fresh.

1) Who is James addressing when he speaks of "teachers"? Of what does he
warn them?

_____

_____

_____

_____

_____

(Verses to consider: Ezek. 33:7–9; Acts 20:26–27; Eph. 4:11–12; Heb. 13:17)

2) According to James, where does the root of the problem of evil speech
lie?

_____

_____

_____

_____

_____

(Verses to consider: Isa. 6:5; Matt. 15:11, 16–19; Mark 7:20–23)

3) What types of evils are caused by the tongue?

_____

_____

_____

_____

(Verses to consider: Ps. 5:9; 34:13; 52:4; Prov. 6:16–17; 26:28)

4) Why are the metaphors James uses for the tongue particularly apt? What do they convey?

_____

_____

_____

_____

_____

_____

GOING DEEPER

Consider what Jesus said about our speech in Matthew 12:33–37.

> **33** *Either make the tree good and its fruit good, or else make the tree bad and its fruit bad; for a tree is known by its fruit.*
>
> **34** *Brood of vipers! How can you, being evil, speak good things? For out of the abundance of the heart the mouth speaks.*
>
> **35** *A good man out of the good treasure of his heart brings forth good things, and an evil man out of the evil treasure brings forth evil things.*
>
> **36** *But I say to you that for every idle word men may speak, they will give account of it in the day of judgment.*
>
> **37** *For by your words you will be justified, and by your words you will be condemned.*

EXPLORING THE MEANING

5) How does Jesus describe the relationship between the heart and the mouth?

_____

_____

_____

_____

_____

_____

6) What eternal perspective does Jesus give on the consequences of our words?

_____

_____

_____

_____

7) Read Psalm 141:3 and Proverbs 21:23. How do we reconcile these verses with James's claim that "no man can tame the tongue"? What is our part and what is God's part?

_____

_____

_____

_____

_____

(Verses to consider: Rom. 6:12–14; Gal. 5:16–26)

Truth for Today

Nowhere is the relationship between faith and works more evident than in a person's speech. What you are will inevitably be disclosed by what you say. It might be said that a person's speech is a reliable measure of his spiritual temperature, a monitor of the inner human condition. The rabbis spoke of the tongue as an arrow rather than a dagger or sword, because it can wound and kill from a great distance. It can wreak great damage even when far from its victim.

Reflecting on the Text

8) Take a few moments for quiet reflection. What recent "transgressions of the tongue" are you aware of? What is the solution for these wrong choices? (Hint: See 1 John 1:9.)

_____

_____

_____

_____

9) C. H. Spurgeon said: "He who speaks with an ill tongue about his neighbor has an ill heart; rest assured of that. Let us engage in our Christian career with the full assurance that we will have a great deal to forgive in other people, but there will be a great deal more to be forgiven in ourselves. Let us count on having to exercise gentleness, and needing its exercise from others. 'Forgiving one another, even as God for Christ's sake hath forgiven you.' " Are there any people you have publicly slandered or maligned? How can you "fix" this situation? What do you need to do? (Hint: See Matt. 5:21–24.)

_____

_____

_____

_____

10) Using the truths and principles you've learned, write down two ways you can avoid sins of speech this next week.

_____

_____

_____

_____

_____

Personal Response

Write out additional reflections, questions you may have, or a prayer.

_____

_____

_____

_____

_____

_____

_____

ADDITIONAL NOTES

8

TRUE WISDOM
James 3:13–18

DRAWING NEAR

Who is the wisest person you know? Explain what you see in that person's life that shows wisdom.

_____

_____

_____

_____

How often does true wisdom really count when we are selecting leaders in the church? Leaders in politics?

_____

_____

_____

_____

What, in your opinion, is the secret to gaining wisdom?

_____

_____

_____

_____

THE CONTEXT

In this passage James makes a transition from discussing teachers and the tongue to dealing with wisdom's impact on everyone's life. He supports the truth revealed in the Old Testament wisdom literature (the book of Job to Song of Solomon) that wisdom is divided into two realms—man's and God's, earthly and heavenly.

James offers wisdom as still another test of living faith. The kind of wisdom a person possesses will be revealed by the kind of life he lives. Those who possess the wisdom of man, the wisdom from below, will demonstrate by their lives that they have no saving relationship with Jesus Christ and no desire to worship, serve, or obey Him. On the other hand, those who possess genuine saving faith will manifest the wisdom of God, the wisdom from above.

Keys to the Text

Wisdom: Both Scripture and ancient philosophers placed a premium on wisdom. Broadly defined, wisdom is not simply a matter of possessing factual knowledge but of properly and effectively applying truth to everyday life. *Sophos* is the common Greek word for speculative knowledge and philosophy, but the Hebrews infused it with the much richer meaning of skillfully applying knowledge to the matter of practical living. The Hebrews to whom James wrote understood that true wisdom was not intellectual, but behavioral. Thus the biggest fool was one who knew truth and failed to apply it. To the Jews, wisdom meant skill in living righteously.

Unleashing the Text

Read James 3:13–18, noting the key words and definitions next to the passage.

James 3:13–18 (NKJV)

understanding (v. 13)—The word for "understanding" is used only here in the New Testament and means a specialist or professional who could skillfully apply his expertise to practical situations. James is asking who is truly skilled in the art of living.

meekness (v. 13)—Also rendered "gentleness," it is the opposite of arrogance and self-promotion; the Greeks described it as power under control.

13 *Who is wise and understanding among you? Let him show by good conduct that his works are done in the meekness of wisdom.*

14 *But if you have bitter envy and self-seeking in your hearts, do not boast and lie against the truth.*

15 *This wisdom does not descend from above, but is earthly, sensual, demonic.*

16 *For where envy and self-seeking exist, confusion and every evil thing are there.*

wisdom (v. 13)—the kind that comes only from God

bitter envy (v. 14)—The Greek term for "bitter" was used of undrinkable water; when combined with "envy" it defines a harsh, resentful attitude toward others.

self-seeking (v. 14)—Sometimes translated "strife," it refers to selfish ambition that engenders antagonism and factionalism. The Greek word came to describe anyone who entered politics for selfish reasons and sought to achieve his agenda at any cost (i.e., even if that meant trampling on others).

from above (v. 15)—Self-centered wisdom that is consumed with personal ambition is not from God.

earthly, sensual, demonic (v. 15)—a description of man's wisdom as: (1) limited to earth; (2) characterized by humanness, frailty, an unsanctified heart, and an unredeemed spirit; and (3) generated by Satan's forces

confusion (v. 16)—This is the disorder that results from the instability and chaos of human wisdom.

17 *But the wisdom that is from above is first pure, then peaceable, gentle, willing to yield, full of mercy and good fruits, without partiality and without hypocrisy.*

18 *Now the fruit of righteousness is sown in peace by those who make peace.*

every evil thing (v. 16)—literally "every worthless [or vile] work." This denotes things that are not so much intrinsically evil as they are simply good for nothing.

pure (v. 17)—This refers to spiritual integrity and moral sincerity; every genuine Christian has this kind of heart motivation.

peaceable (v. 17)—means "peace loving" or "peace promoting"

gentle (v. 17)—This word is difficult to translate, but most nearly means a character trait of sweet reasonableness. Such a person will submit to all kinds of mistreatment and difficulty with an attitude of kind, courteous, patient humility, without any thought of hatred or revenge (see Matt. 5:10–11).

willing to yield (v. 17)—The original term described someone who was teachable, compliant, easily persuaded, and who willingly submitted to military discipline or moral and legal standards; for believers, it defines obedience to God's standards (see Matt. 5:3–5).

full of mercy (v. 17)—the gift of showing concern for those who suffer pain and hardship, and the ability to forgive quickly (see Matt. 5:7)

without partiality (v. 17)—The Greek word occurs only here in the New Testament and denotes a consistent, unwavering person who is undivided in his commitment and conviction and does not make unfair distinctions.

fruit of righteousness (v. 18)—good works that result from salvation (see v. 17)

those who make peace (v. 18)—Righteousness flourishes in a climate of spiritual peace.

1) How do we show that we are wise?

_____

_____

_____

_____

2) How is godly wisdom described and defined in this passage?

_____

_____

_____

_____

_____

(Verses to consider: Job 28; Ps. 104:24; Prov. 1:7; Dan. 1:17; Rom. 11:33)

3) What did James mean when he referred to the "meekness of wisdom" (v. 13)?

_____

_____

_____

_____

_____

(Verses to consider: Matt. 5:5; Gal. 5:22–23)

4) List all the "fruits" of earthly wisdom and heavenly wisdom that James mentions. Compare and contrast them. How are they different? What are the results/consequences of each?

_____

_____

_____

_____

(Verses to consider: Matt. 5:6; 1 Cor. 1:18–31; 2:6–16; Gal. 5:22–23; Phil. 1:11)

5) What does it mean that God's wisdom is "pure" (v. 17)?

_____

_____

_____

_____

(Verses to consider: Ps. 24:3–4; Matt. 5:8)

GOING DEEPER

To learn more about godly wisdom, read Proverbs 2:1–7, penned by King Solomon.

1 *My son, if you receive my words, and treasure my commands within you,*
2 *So that you incline your ear to wisdom, and apply your heart to understanding;*
3 *Yes, if you cry out for discernment, and lift up your voice for understanding,*
4 *If you seek her as silver, and search for her as for hidden treasures;*

5   *Then you will understand the fear of the LORD, and find the knowledge of God.*

6   *For the LORD gives wisdom; from His mouth come knowledge and understanding;*

7   *He stores up sound wisdom for the upright; he is a shield to those who walk uprightly.*

EXPLORING THE MEANING

6) Circle all the synonyms used for "wisdom" in this passage. What do these terms reveal about the nature of wisdom?

_____

_____

_____

_____

7) What is the source of true wisdom? How do we get it?

_____

_____

_____

_____

8) Read Colossians 2:2–3. What does this passage say about Christ and wisdom?

_____

_____

_____

_____

TRUTH FOR TODAY

If a person professes saving faith in Jesus Christ and claims to have wisdom from God, but has a heart that is proud, arrogant, and self-centered and lives a life that is worldly, sensual, and self-serving, his claims to salvation are false. He is lying against the truth.

Reflecting on the Text

9) How can a person tell if the wisdom he/she is receiving is man's or God's?

_____

_____

_____

_____

10) To what degree does the world's wisdom hold sway over your thoughts, opinions, and values? Why?

_____

_____

_____

_____

11) What are some concrete ways a Christian can acquire God's wisdom? Try to list ten. Circle the ones you regularly practice. Put a check mark by the activities that need to become part of your daily experience.

_____

_____

_____

_____

12) What can you do today to become more passionate about pursuing God's wisdom and seeking it like treasure?

_____

_____

_____

_____

Personal Response

Write out additional reflections, questions you may have, or a prayer.

_____

_____

_____

_____

_____

_____

_____

_____

_____

_____

_____

_____

_____

_____

_____

_____

_____

_____

_____

_____

_____

_____

_____

_____

_____

_____

_____

ADDITIONAL NOTES

9

FRIENDSHIP WITH THE WORLD
James 4:1–12

DRAWING NEAR

How do you define "worldliness"?

_____

_____

_____

_____

Give some examples of activities that some Christians might typically view as "worldly."

_____

_____

_____

_____

How do we live "in" the world but not "of" the world?

_____

_____

_____

_____

THE CONTEXT

We've seen James examine a number of everyday behaviors that can serve either to authenticate one's claim to faith or highlight the absence of true saving faith. Now he addresses one's attitude toward the world. The central truth in this passage is, "Friendship with the world is enmity with God" (4:4). James argues persuasively that genuine spiritual life and faithful Christian living involve separation from the world and all its countless contaminations. Conversely, a continuing, habitual friendship with the world is grounded in human wisdom and is evidence of unbelief. Such a lifestyle invariably leads to interpersonal conflict.

This passage admonishes readers to intentionally withdraw from their friendship with the world. As you study this lesson, ask God to help you put away any remaining vestiges of worldly living that might be impeding your spiritual growth. How? By humbly drawing near to Him.

KEYS TO THE TEXT

The World: The Greek word used here is *Kosmos*. It does not refer to the physical earth or universe but rather to the spiritual reality of the man-centered, Satan-directed system of this present age, which is hostile to God and God's people. It refers to the self-centered, godless value system and moral contamination of fallen mankind. The goal of the world is self-glory, self-fulfillment, self-indulgence, self-satisfaction, and every other form of self-serving, all of which amounts to hostility toward God. While the world's philosophies and ideologies and much that it offers may appear attractive and appealing, that is deception. Its true and pervasive nature is evil, harmful, ruinous, and satanic. God, not the world, must have the first place in the Christian's life (see 1 John 2:15).

UNLEASHING THE TEXT

Read James 4:1–12, noting the key words and definitions next to the passage.

James 4:1–12 (NKJV)

wars and fights . . . among you (v. 1)—These are between people in the church, not internal conflict in individual people. "Wars" speaks of the conflict in general; "fights" of its specific manifestations. Discord in the church is not by God's design, but results from the mix of tares (false believers) and wheat (truly redeemed people) that make up the church.

1 *Where do wars and fights come from among you? Do they not come from your desires for pleasure that war in your members?*

2 *You lust and do not have. You murder and covet and cannot obtain. You fight and war. Yet you do not have because you do not ask.*

desires (v. 1)—The Greek word (from which the English word "hedonism" derives) always has a negative connotation in the New Testament; the passionate desires for worldly pleasures that mark unbelievers (1:14) are the internal source of the external conflict in the church (see James 1:14–15).

your members (v. 1)—not church members, but bodily members (see Rom. 6:13). James, like Paul, uses "members" to speak of sinful, fallen human nature (see Rom. 6:19); unbelievers (who are in view here) fight (unsuccessfully) against the evil desires they cannot control.

murder (v. 2)—the ultimate result of thwarted desires. James had in mind actual murder, and the gamut of sins (hate, anger, bitterness) leading up to it. The picture is of unbelievers so driven by their uncontrollable evil desires that they will fight to the death to fulfill them.

you do not ask (v. 2)—True joy, peace, happiness, meaning, hope, and fulfillment in life come only from God; unbelievers, however, are unwilling to ask for them on His terms—they refuse to submit to God or acknowledge their dependence on Him.

3 *You ask and do not receive, because you ask amiss, that you may spend it on your pleasures.*

4 *Adulterers and adulteresses! Do you not know that friendship with the world is enmity with God? Whoever therefore wants to be a friend of the world makes himself an enemy of God.*

5 *Or do you think that the Scripture says in vain, "The Spirit who dwells in us yearns jealously"?*

6 *But He gives more grace. Therefore He says: "God resists the proud, but gives grace to the humble."*

7 *Therefore submit to God. Resist the devil and he will flee from you.*

amiss (v. 3)—This refers to acting in an evil manner, motivated by personal gratification and selfish desire; unbelievers seek things for their own pleasures, not the honor and glory of God.

Adulterers and adulteresses! (v. 4)—This metaphorical description of spiritual unfaithfulness would have been especially familiar to James's Jewish readers, since the Old Testament often describes unfaithful Israel as a spiritual harlot (see Hos. 9:1). James has in view professing Christians, outwardly associated with the church, but holding a deep affection for the evil world system.

friendship (v. 4)—Appearing only here in the New Testament, the Greek word describes love in the sense of a strong emotional attachment; those with a deep and intimate longing for the things of the world give evidence that they are not redeemed.

enmity with God (v. 4)—the necessary corollary to friendship with the world. The sobering truth that unbelievers are God's enemies is taught throughout Scripture (see Deut. 32:41–43).

Scripture says (v. 5)—a common New Testament way of introducing an Old Testament quote (John 19:37; Rom. 4:3; 9:17; 10:11; 11:2; Gal. 4:30; 1 Tim. 5:18). The quote that follows, however, is not found as such in the Old Testament, but it is a composite of general Old Testament teaching.

The Spirit . . . yearns jealously (v. 5)—This difficult phrase is best understood by seeing the "spirit" as a reference not to the Holy Spirit, but to the human spirit, and translating the phrase "yearns jealously" in the negative sense of "lusts to envy." James's point is that an unbelieving person's spirit (inner person) is bent on evil; those who think otherwise defy the biblical diagnosis of fallen human nature; and those who live in worldly lusts give evidence that their faith is not genuine (see Rom. 8:5–11; 1 Cor. 2:14).

more grace (v. 6)—The only ray of hope in man's spiritual darkness is the sovereign grace of God, which alone can rescue man from his propensity to lust for evil things. That God gives "more grace" shows that His grace is greater than the power of sin, the flesh, the world, and Satan (see Rom. 5:20). The Old Testament quote (from Prov. 3:34) reveals who obtains God's grace—the humble, not the proud enemies of God. The word "humble" does not define a special class of Christians, but encompasses all believers (see Isa. 57:15; Matt. 18:3–4).

submit (v. 7)—Literally "to line up under," the word was used of soldiers under the authority of their commander. In the New Testament, it describes Jesus' submission to His parents' authority (Luke 2:51), submission to human government (Rom. 13:1), the church's submission to Christ (Eph. 5:24), and servants' submission to their masters (Titus 2:9; 1 Pet. 2:18). James used the word to describe a willing, conscious submission to God's authority as sovereign Ruler of the universe. A truly humble person will give his allegiance to God, obey His commands, and follow His leadership.

Resist the devil and he will flee from you. (v. 7)—the flip side of the first command. "Resist" literally means "take your stand against." All people are either under the lordship of Christ or the lordship of Satan; there is no middle ground. Those who transfer their allegiance from Satan to God will find that Satan "will flee from" them since he is a defeated foe.

Draw near (v. 8)—pursue an intimate love relationship with God. The concept of drawing near to God was associated originally with the Levitical priests (Lev. 10:3; Ezek. 44:13), but eventually came to describe anyone's approach to God. Salvation involves more than submitting to God and resisting the devil; the redeemed heart longs for communion with God (Ps. 42:1–2).

Cleanse your hands (v. 8)—The Old Testament priests had to ceremonially wash their hands before approaching God, and sinners (a term used only for unbelievers) who would approach Him must recognize and confess their sin.

8 Draw near to God and He will draw near to you. Cleanse your hands, you sinners; and purify your hearts, you double-minded.

9 Lament and mourn and weep! Let your laughter be turned to mourning and your joy to gloom.

10 Humble yourselves in the sight of the Lord, and He will lift you up.

11 Do not speak evil of one another, brethren. He who speaks evil of a brother and judges his brother, speaks evil of the law and judges the law. But if you judge the law, you are not a doer of the law but a judge.

12 There is one Lawgiver, who is able to save and to destroy. Who are you to judge another?

purify your hearts (v. 8)—Cleansing the hands symbolizes external behavior; this phrase refers to the inner thoughts, motives, and desires of the heart.

Lament (v. 9)—be afflicted, wretched, and miserable. This is the state of those truly broken over their sin.

mourn (v. 9)—God will not turn away a heart broken and contrite over sin (2 Cor. 7:10); mourning is the inner response to such brokenness.

weep (v. 9)—the outward manifestation of inner sorrow over sin

laughter (v. 9)—Used only here in the New Testament, the word signifies the flippant laughter of those foolishly indulging in worldly pleasures. The picture is of people who give no thought to God, life, death, sin, judgment, or holiness. James calls on such people to mourn over their sin (see Luke 18:13–14).

speak evil (v. 11)—This means to slander or defame. James does not forbid confronting those in sin, which is elsewhere commanded in Scripture (Matt. 18:15–17; Titus 1:13; 2:15; 3:10); rather, he condemns careless, derogatory, critical, slanderous accusations against others (see Ps. 50:20; Prov. 10:18; Rom. 1:29; Titus 2:3).

speaks evil of a brother . . . speaks evil of the law (v. 11)—Those who speak evil of other believers set themselves up as judges and condemn them (see 2:4). They thereby defame and disregard God's law, which expressly forbids such slanderous condemnation.

judges the law (v. 11)—By refusing to submit to the law, slanderers place themselves above it as its judges.

one Lawgiver (v. 12)—God, who gave the law (see Isa. 33:22); He alone has the authority to save those who repent from its penalty and destroy those who refuse to repent.

1) Why is James so intolerant of conflict in the church? What causes this infighting?

_____

_____

_____

_____

_____

(Verses to consider: John 17:20–21; 2 Cor. 12:20; Eph. 2:3; 2 Tim. 3:2–5)

2) Why does James address some of his readers as "adulterers and adulteresses"? What does this phrase mean?

_____

_____

_____

_____

_____

3) What does it mean to be friends with the world? What does it mean to be at enmity with God (v. 4)?

_____

_____

_____

_____

(Verses to consider: Ps. 21:8; Isa. 42:13; Nah. 1:2, 8; Luke 19:27; Rom. 5:10; 1 Cor. 15:25)

4) What should be the Christian's relationship with the world?

_____

_____

_____

_____

(Verses to consider: 1 John 2:15–17)

5) Summarize the remedy James gives for being restored to God (vv. 6–10).

_____

_____

_____

_____

6) Why is James so adamant about not slandering and judging others? Does this mean that believers are forbidden to confront overt sin in others? Why or why not?

_____

_____

_____

_____

(Verses to consider: Prov. 10:18; 11:9; 1 Cor. 4:14;
2 Cor. 12:20; Eph. 4:31; Col. 1:28; 2 Tim. 3:3; Titus 2:3)

GOING DEEPER

To avoid the world, we must seek God and make Him first in our lives. To find out more about how to do that, read what David, the psalmist, wrote in Psalm 63:1–11.

1 *O God, You are my God; early will I seek You; my soul thirsts for You; my flesh longs for You in a dry and thirsty land where there is no water.*
2 *So I have looked for You in the sanctuary, to see Your power and Your glory.*
3 *Because Your lovingkindness is better than life, my lips shall praise You.*
4 *Thus I will bless You while I live; I will lift up my hands in Your name.*
5 *My soul shall be satisfied as with marrow and fatness, and my mouth shall praise You with joyful lips.*
6 *When I remember You on my bed, I meditate on You in the night watches.*
7 *Because You have been my help, therefore in the shadow of Your wings I will rejoice.*
8 *My soul follows close behind You; Your right hand upholds me.*

9 *But those who seek my life, to destroy it, shall go into the lower parts of the earth.*

10 *They shall fall by the sword; they shall be a portion for jackals.*

11 *But the king shall rejoice in God; everyone who swears by Him shall glory; but the mouth of those who speak lies shall be stopped.*

EXPLORING THE MEANING

7) Look at all the actions and verbs used here to describe the psalmist's relationship with God. What does this passage teach you about drawing near to God?

_____

_____

_____

_____

_____

(Verses to consider: Ps. 27:8; 73:28; Heb. 4:16)

8) In what ways is the passion and desire for God displayed in this psalm a mark of a true believer?

_____

_____

_____

_____

_____

9) Read Psalm 24:3–4. What are the prerequisites to drawing near to God?

_____

_____

_____

_____

_____

(Verses to consider: Ezek. 18:31; 36:25–26; 2 Tim. 2:22; 1 Pet. 1:22)

10) Read John 8:44. What is the relationship between unbelievers and Satan? What will it mean to "resist the devil" as James said?

_____

_____

_____

_____

_____

(Verses to consider: Eph. 2:2; 1 John 3:8; 5:19)

TRUTH FOR TODAY

Friendship with the world and friendship with God are mutually exclusive. Christians have a nature so utterly distinct from the lovers of the world, the followers of Satan, that they should never entertain any of the ways or hold any of the loyalties that characterize unbelievers. For believers to pursue worldly things goes against the grain of their new nature, and they cannot be comfortable or satisfied until they renounce those things and return to their first love.

REFLECTING ON THE TEXT

11) How do your actions reveal where your true affections lie? In what ways are you too enamored with the things of this world?

_____

_____

_____

_____

12) In verses 2 and 3 James addresses the issue of improper motives in the prayers of unbelievers. Examine your own prayer life. How much of your prayer life is focused on selfish desires? How can you change this?

_____

_____

_____

_____

13) Spend a few minutes meditating on James 4:11–12. How careful are you when speaking about others? What do you sense God is telling you from this passage?

_____

_____

_____

_____

_____

_____

PERSONAL RESPONSE

Write out additional reflections, questions you may have, or a prayer.

_____

_____

_____

_____

_____

_____

_____

_____

_____

_____

_____

_____

_____

_____

_____

ADDITIONAL NOTES

10

RESPONDING TO THE WILL OF GOD
James 4:13–17

DRAWING NEAR

How do you define the phrase "the will of God"?

_____

_____

_____

Describe some ways you've seen other Christians discern God's will.

_____

_____

_____

_____

How do *you* go about determining God's will for your life? Why?

_____

_____

_____

THE CONTEXT

For James, doing the will of God identifies another test of genuine saving faith. True Christians are characterized as "doing the will of God from the heart" (Eph. 6:6). They joyfully, willingly pray, "Your kingdom come, Your will be done" (Matt. 6:10).

On the other hand, a constant disregard for or lack of interest in God's will is a certain mark of the presence of pride—the ugly sin also underlying conflict, worldliness, and slander (4:1–12). To disregard God's will is tantamount to saying, "I am the sovereign ruler of my own life." Such a prideful attitude is antithetical to saving faith. As James has already pointed out, "God resists the proud, but gives grace to the humble" (4:6).

True to the pattern he has followed throughout his epistle, James takes a practical approach to the issue of responding to God's will. In this brief passage James gives significant insights into the ways people respond to God's will.

Keys to the Text

God's Will: In the broadest sense, God's will is expressed in all the commands and principles of Scripture. Specifically, the Bible says that God's will is that people be saved (1 Tim. 2:4; 2 Pet. 3:9), Spirit-filled (Eph. 5:17–18), sanctified (1 Thess. 4:3–8), submissive (1 Pet. 2:13–15), and suffering (1 Pet. 3:17). For the Christian, doing God's will is an act of worship (Rom. 12:1–2). It is to be done from the heart (Eph. 6:6) as a way of life (Col. 1:9–10; 4:12), recognizing that He must energize us to do it (Heb. 13:20–21). Acknowledging God's will affirms His sovereignty over all aspects of life. We live only because God so wills it, for He controls life and death.

Unleashing the Text

Read James 4:13–17, noting the key words and definitions next to the passage.

James 4:13–17 (NKJV)

"Today or tomorrow . . . " (v. 13)—James does not condemn wise business planning, but rather planning that leaves out God; the people so depicted are practical atheists, living their lives and making their plans as if God did not exist. Such conduct is inconsistent with genuine saving faith, which submits to God.

know what will happen (v. 14)—James exposes the presumptuous folly of the practical atheists he condemned in v. 13. They do not know what the future holds for them; God alone knows the future.

13 *Come now, you who say, "Today or tomorrow we will go to such and such a city, spend a year there, buy and sell, and make a profit";*

14 *whereas you do not know what will happen tomorrow. For what is your life? It is even a vapor that appears for a little time and then vanishes away.*

15 *Instead you ought to say, "If the Lord wills, we shall live and do this or that."*

16 *But now you boast in your arrogance. All such boasting is evil.*

17 *Therefore, to him who knows to do good and does not do it, to him it is sin.*

vapor (v. 14)—This refers either to a puff of smoke or one's breath that appears for a moment in cold air. It stresses the transitory nature of life (see 1:10; Job 7:6–7).

the Lord wills (v. 15)—The true Christian submits his plans to the lordship of Christ (see v. 7).

boasting (v. 16)—arrogant bragging about their anticipated business accomplishments

sin (v. 17)—The implication is that they also did what they shouldn't do; sins of omission lead directly to sins of commission.

1) How does James characterize our lives (i.e., the length of our lives)? Why is this significant?

_____

_____

_____

_____

(Verses to consider: Job 9:25–26; Ps. 39:5, 11; 62:9; 90:5–6, 10)

2) Why does James insist that we preface our plans by saying, "If the Lord wills . . ."? What does this mindset indicate?

_____

_____

_____

_____

_____

(Verses to consider: Prov. 19:21; Acts 18:21; Rom. 1:10; 1 Cor. 4:19)

3) How does a concern for the will of God demonstrate our belief in His sovereignty?

_____

_____

_____

_____

_____

(Verses to consider: Deut. 32:39; Job 12:9–10; Ps. 104:29; Heb. 9:27)

4) According to James, what lies behind the reasoning that excludes God and His will?

_____

_____

_____

_____

GOING DEEPER

To get Jesus' perspective on the uncertainty of life, read Luke 12:13–21.

13 *Then one from the crowd said to Him, "Teacher, tell my brother to divide the inheritance with me."*

14 *But He said to him, "Man, who made Me a judge or an arbitrator over you?"*

15 *And He said to them, "Take heed and beware of covetousness, for one's life does not consist in the abundance of the things he possesses."*

16 *Then He spoke a parable to them, saying: "The ground of a certain rich man yielded plentifully.*

17 *And he thought within himself, saying, 'What shall I do, since I have no room to store my crops?'*

18 *So he said, 'I will do this: I will pull down my barns and build greater, and there I will store all my crops and my goods.*

19 *And I will say to my soul, "Soul, you have many goods laid up for many years; take your ease; eat, drink, and be merry." '*

20 *But God said to him, 'Fool! This night your soul will be required of you; then whose will those things be which you have provided?'*

21 *"So is he who lays up treasure for himself, and is not rich toward God."*

EXPLORING THE MEANING

5) What does this parable teach you about priorities? about wealth? about certainties in life?

_____

_____

_____

_____

6) Read Proverbs 27:1. Why is it foolish to presume on the future?

_____

_____

_____

_____

7) Read Isaiah 46:9–10. What does this passage say about God and the future?

_____

_____

_____

_____

TRUTH FOR TODAY

The Scriptures give many marks of a true Christian, such as love for God, repentance from sin, humility, devotion to God's glory, prayer, love for others, separation from the world, growth, and obedience. But nothing more clearly summarizes the character of a genuine believer than a desire to do the will of God.

REFLECTING ON THE TEXT

8) What are some things that you know are clearly the will of God?

_____

_____

_____

_____

_____

(Verses to consider: Eph. 5:17–21; 1 Thess. 4:3–8; 1 Pet. 2:13–15; 3:17)

9) Ponder your approach to a typical day. How much does God and His will figure into your plans? Is His kingdom and His righteousness (Matt. 6:33) foremost in your thoughts? Or are spiritual realities shoved into the margins of your life as an afterthought?

_____

_____

_____

_____

_____

10) How can you become more focused on knowing and doing the will of God?

_____

_____

_____

_____

11) Someone has said that about 90 percent of God's will for our lives is already revealed in the Bible. In other words, God has already unveiled what should be the primary direction of our lives, and as we obey those broad principles, He makes the details clear. If this is true, then a careful study and knowledge of Scripture is imperative for believers. Consider your own spiritual habits. How much time per week do you spend in:

~ hearing God's Word read/preached/taught?

~ reading God's Word?

~ studying God's Word (digging deeper into specific passages)?

~ memorizing God's Word?

~ meditating on God's Word (letting the truths of Scripture permeate deeply into your heart and mind)?

12) As you ponder your response to the above question, write out two changes you need to make in your schedule this week to spend more time in God's Word.

_____

_____

_____

_____

_____

_____

Personal Response

Write out additional reflections, questions you may have, or a prayer.

_____

_____

_____

_____

_____

_____

_____

_____

_____

_____

_____

_____

_____

_____

_____

_____

_____

_____

_____

_____

_____

_____

_____

_____

_____

ADDITIONAL NOTES

11

RICHES, TRIALS, AND OATHS
James 5:1–12

DRAWING NEAR

Some Christians insist that it is an overt sin for North American believers to drive expensive foreign cars when people (and especially fellow Christians) around the world are starving to death. Others look unfavorably on Western Christians who live in luxurious homes or who take extravagant vacations. Are these advocates of frugal living correct? Why or why not?

_____

_____

_____

Would you consider yourself materialistic? Why or why not?

_____

_____

_____

_____

In courtrooms every day, witnesses place their hand on the Bible and swear to tell the truth, the whole truth, and nothing but the truth. Is this a Christian practice or not? Why do you think so?

_____

_____

_____

_____

THE CONTEXT

As noted throughout this study, James's goal is to present various tests of genuine saving faith. Building on the teachings of Jesus, James presents a blistering denunciation of those who profess to worship God but in fact worship money. His rebuke of the wicked wealthy is in keeping with the tradition of the Old Testament prophets. James tells them to examine the true state of their hearts in light of how they feel about wealth.

He then shifts his focus to the topic of persecution, instructing the folks who are suffering at the hands of the rich and powerful to be patient and keep perspective. Verse 12 then touches on another custom during biblical times—that of swearing oaths. This practice had become an issue in the church, particularly since swearing oaths was an integral part of Jewish culture and Jewish believers comprised a large segment of the early church. James commands them not to swear oaths and encourages believers to be distinctive in speaking the truth.

KEYS TO THE TEXT

Oaths: Old Testament law prescribed oaths in certain circumstances (Num. 5:19, 21; 30:2–3). God confirmed a promise with an oath (Heb. 6:13–18; cf. Acts 2:30). Christ Himself spoke under oath (26:63–64). Therefore, James's command to not swear an oath should not be taken as a universal condemnation of oaths in all circumstances. What James forbids here is the flippant, profane, or careless use of oaths in everyday speech. In that culture, Jews would swear by "heaven," "earth," "Jerusalem," or their own "heads," not by God. As Jesus did before him, James condemned the practice of swearing false, evasive, deceptive oaths by everything other than the name of the Lord (which alone was considered binding). Jesus suggested that all our speech should be as if we were under an oath to tell the truth (see Matt. 5:34–37).

UNLEASHING THE TEXT

Read James 5:1–12, noting the key words and definitions next to the passage.

rich (v. 1)—those with more than they need to live. James condemns them not for being wealthy, but for misusing their resources. Unlike the believing rich in Timothy's congregation (1 Tim. 6:17–19), these are the wicked wealthy who profess Christian faith and have associated themselves with the church, but whose real god is money. For prostituting the goodness and generosity of God, they can anticipate only divine punishment (v. 5).

James 5:1–12 (NKJV)

1 Come now, you rich, weep and howl for your miseries that are coming upon you!

2 Your riches are corrupted, and your garments are moth-eaten.

3 Your gold and silver are corroded, and their corrosion will be a witness against you and will eat your flesh like fire. You have heaped up treasure in the last days.

corrupted . . . motheaten . . . corroded (vv. 2–3)—James points out the folly of hoarding food, expensive clothing, or money—all of which is subject to decay, theft, fire, or other forms of loss.

last days (v. 3)—the period between Christ's first and second comings. James rebukes the rich for living as if Jesus were never coming back.

4 *Indeed the wages of the laborers who mowed your fields, which you kept back by fraud, cry out; and the cries of the reapers have reached the ears of the Lord of Sabaoth.*

5 *You have lived on the earth in pleasure and luxury; you have fattened your hearts as in a day of slaughter.*

6 *You have condemned, you have murdered the just; he does not resist you.*

7 *Therefore be patient, brethren, until the coming of the Lord. See how the farmer waits for the precious fruit of the earth, waiting patiently for it until it receives the early and latter rain.*

8 *You also be patient. Establish your hearts, for the coming of the Lord is at hand.*

9 *Do not grumble against one another, brethren, lest you be condemned. Behold, the Judge is standing at the door!*

wages . . . you kept back (v. 4)—The rich had gained some of their wealth by oppressing and defrauding their day laborers—a practice strictly forbidden in the Old Testament (see Lev. 19:13; Deut. 24:14–15).

the Lord of Sabaoth (v. 4)—an untranslated Greek word meaning "hosts"; the One who hears the cries of the defrauded laborers, James warns, is the Lord of hosts (a name for God used frequently in the Old Testament), the commander of the armies of heaven (angels).

pleasure and luxury (v. 5)—After robbing their workers to accumulate their wealth, the rich indulged themselves in an extravagant lifestyle. "Pleasure" has the connotation of wanton pleasure. "Luxury" leads to vice when a person becomes consumed with the pursuit of pleasure, since a life without self-denial soon becomes out of control in every area.

a day of slaughter (v. 5)—Like fattened cattle ready to be slaughtered, the rich that James condemns had indulged themselves to the limit. This is a vivid depiction of divine judgment, in keeping with the metaphor likening the overindulgent rich to fattened cattle.

condemned . . . murdered (v. 6)—This describes the next step in the sinful progression of the rich. Hoarding led to fraud, which led to self-indulgence; finally, that overindulgence had consumed the rich to the point that they would do anything to sustain their lifestyle. "Condemned" comes from a word meaning "to sentence"; the implication is that the rich were using the courts to commit judicial murder (see 2:6).

patient (v. 7)—The word emphasizes patience with people (see 1 Thess. 5:14), rather than in trials or difficult circumstances (as in 1:3); specifically, James has in mind patience with the oppressive rich.

the coming (v. 7)—the second coming of Christ. Realizing the glory that awaits them at Christ's return should motivate believers to patiently endure mistreatment.

the early and latter rain (v. 7)—The "early" rain falls in Israel during October and November and softens the ground for planting; the "latter" rain falls in March and April, immediately before the spring harvest. Just as the farmer waits patiently from the early rain to the latter for his crop to ripen, so must Christians patiently wait for the Lord's return (see Gal. 6:9; 2 Tim. 4:8; Titus 2:13).

Establish your hearts (v. 8)—This is a call for resolute, firm courage and commitment. James exhorts those about to collapse under the weight of persecution to shore up their hearts with the hope of the Second Coming.

at hand (v. 8)—The imminency of Christ's return is a frequent theme in the New Testament.

Do not grumble . . . the Judge is standing at the door! (v. 9)—James pictured Christ as a judge about to open the doors to the courtroom and convene His court. Knowing that the strain of persecution could lead to grumbling, James cautioned his readers against that sin, lest they forfeit their full reward.

the perseverance of Job (v. 11)—Job is the classic example of a man who patiently endured suffering and was blessed by God for his persevering faith; James reassured his readers that God had a purpose for their suffering, just as He did for Job's.

compassionate and merciful (v. 11)—Remembering the Lord's character is a great comfort in suffering. The Scriptures repeatedly affirm His compassion and mercy (see Ps. 25:6; 103:8, 13; 116:5; 136:1; 145:8).

10 *My brethren, take the prophets, who spoke in the name of the Lord, as an example of suffering and patience.*

11 *Indeed we count them blessed who endure. You have heard of the perseverance of Job and seen the end intended by the Lord—that the Lord is very compassionate and merciful.*

12 *But above all, my brethren, do not swear, either by heaven or by earth or with any other oath. But let your "Yes" be "Yes," and your "No," "No," lest you fall into judgment.*

above all (v. 12)—or "especially." As he has done repeatedly in his epistle, James stressed that a person's speech provides the most revealing glimpse of his spiritual condition (see 1:26; 2:12; 3:2–11; 4:11).

"Yes" be "Yes" (v. 12)—Echoing Jesus' words, James called for straightforward, honest, plain speech; to speak otherwise is to invite God's judgment.

1) What charges does James bring against the wealthy? Why was he so harsh in his rebuke?

_____

_____

_____

_____

_____

(Verses to consider: Isa. 10:1–4; Amos 4:1–3; Matt. 6:19–21)

2) Does James teach that it is a sin to be wealthy? How do you support your answer?

_____

_____

_____

_____

_____

(Verses to consider: Deut. 8:18; Prov. 10:22)

3) How does James counsel his readers to respond in times of trouble? Why?

_____

_____

_____

_____

_____

(Verses to consider: 2 Cor. 4:17; 1 Pet. 1: 6–7; 2:21–23; 4:7)

4) What were they to learn from Job's example of suffering?

_____

_____

_____

_____

_____

5) What did James teach about Christ's return (vv. 8–9)?

_____

_____

_____

_____

_____

(Verses to consider: Rom. 13:12; Heb. 10:25; 1 Pet. 4:7; 1 John 2:18)

6) Why did James argue that the Jewish custom of swearing oaths was unnecessary and improper in the church?

_____

_____

_____

_____

_____

(Verses to consider: Matt. 5:33–37; Eph. 4:25; Col. 3:9)

Going Deeper

James's sharp rebuke of the wicked wealthy is in keeping with the tradition of the Old Testament prophets. Read the prophet Isaiah's warnings to those who misused their wealth in Isaiah 3:14–15 and 10:1–4.

> 3:14 *The Lord will enter into judgment with the elders of His people and His princes: "For you have eaten up the vineyard; the plunder of the poor is in your houses.*
> 15 *"What do you mean by crushing My people and grinding the faces of the poor?" says the Lord God of hosts. . . .*
>
> 10:1 *"Woe to those who decree unrighteous decrees, who write misfortune, which they have prescribed*
> 2 *"To rob the needy of justice, and to take what is right from the poor of My people, that widows may be their prey, and that they may rob the fatherless.*
> 3 *"What will you do in the day of punishment, and in the desolation which will come from afar? To whom will you flee for help? And where will you leave your glory?*
> 4 *"Without Me they shall bow down among the prisoners, and they shall fall among the slain." For all this His anger is not turned away, but His hand is stretched out still.*

Exploring the Meaning

7) What charges did Isaiah bring against the wealthy elders and princes?

_____

_____

_____

_____

8) What do you learn about God from this passage in Isaiah?

_____

_____

_____

_____

9) Read 1 Tim. 6:10, 17–19. What do you learn here about a proper view and use of money?

_____

_____

_____

_____

Truth for Today

The Bible does not teach that possessing wealth is sinful in and of itself. What *is* wrong is to misuse one's wealth. Wealth may be a blessing, a gift from God bringing the opportunity to do good. But that can only be true of those who are also "rich in faith" (James 2:5) and "rich toward God" (Luke 12:21). If wealth is to be a source of blessing and not condemnation, it must not be uselessly hoarded, unjustly gained, self-indulgently spent, or ruthlessly acquired.

Reflecting on the Text

10) Which do you have to watch out for most in your own life: acquiring riches ruthlessly or unjustly, hoarding money uselessly, or spending wealth self-indulgently? What needs to change in your view of wealth and how to handle it?

_____

_____

_____

_____

11) Different people respond differently to trials. Some become quiet, philosophical, even resigned. Others become sad, hopeless, and despondent; still others become angry and bitter. Some, though, put their hope in God and maintain a tangible joy despite their circumstances. What description best characterizes you in times of difficulty? Explain.

_____

_____

_____

_____

12) Why is it always comforting and wise to remember God's character in times of difficulty?

_____

_____

_____

_____

13) People sometimes try to make their promises more convincing by using phrases such as: "Cross my heart!" or "I swear to you/to God!" or "I'm not kidding—trust me! If I don't keep my word then you can . . ."? How, if at all, does James 5:12 speak to these kinds of exclamations?

_____

_____

_____

_____

14) Why do we struggle with just letting our "yes" be "yes" and our "no" be "no"? Ask God to help you honor Him this week by speaking with integrity.

_____

_____

_____

_____

PERSONAL RESPONSE

Write out additional reflections, questions you may have, or a prayer.

_____

_____

_____

_____

_____

_____

12

RIGHTEOUS PRAYING
James 5:13–20

DRAWING NEAR

Different people respond differently to difficulties and suffering. How do
the unbelievers you know typically respond? How do the most mature
Christians you know respond? How do *you* usually respond?

_____

_____

_____

_____

When was the last time you confessed your sin to another person and had
them pray with or for you regarding that sin? Why do many believers find
this difficult—often to the point of not doing it at all?

_____

_____

_____

_____

THE CONTEXT

As we come to this final passage, it would be surprising, if, in this letter to
struggling, persecuted believers, James neglected to mention prayer. A strong
commitment to prayer is a prerequisite to enduring suffering and affliction.
James's exhortation to prayer embraces the prayer life of the entire church.
Individual believers are called to pray in verse 13, the elders in verses 14–15, and
the congregation in verse 16.

This section also reflects James's compassionate pastoral care for his
suffering flock; his main focus is on the casualties of the spiritual battle—the
persecuted, weak, defeated believers. As the context and content of this section
make clear, the subject is not physical illness or healing. Instead, its concern
is with healing spiritual weakness, spiritual weariness, spiritual exhaustion, and
spiritual depression through prayer, as well as dealing with the suffering and sin
that accompanies it.

The final two verses form a fitting conclusion to the book of James. They express James's primary objective in writing his epistle: to confront those in the assembly of believers who possessed a false, dead faith. Here is one last salvation warning regarding those who identify with the church but are not regenerate. But rather than speaking directly to them, James calls on the genuine Christians in the church to do evangelism. He wants the believers to pursue the "make-believers."

Keys to the Text

Prayer: Fellowship and communion with God involving adoration, worship, praise, thanksgiving, supplication, petition, confession, repentance, meditation, dedication, and intercession. Christian prayer addresses God as Father through and in the name of Jesus Christ His Son, and is based on the confidence that He hears His children. Prayer is drawn partly from the urgency of human needs and partly from the promise and challenge of God's Word. Personal prayer is shaped by the awareness of God's presence. Corporate prayer is the living breath of the church. Through prayer, the church resists the assaults of Satan (Matt. 26:41; Eph. 6:13–20), receives the gifts of grace (Acts 4:31), seeks deliverance, healing, and restoration for the saints (Eph. 6:18; James 5:15; 1 John 5:16), supports evangelization (Col. 4:3–4), and hastens the return of the Lord (Rev. 22:20). (*Nelson's New Christian Dictionary*)

Anointing with Oil: This meant literally "rubbing with oil." In Bible times priests were anointed for entry into service. In addition, olive oil was often used medicinally as a healing agent (see Mark 6:13). James's use could possibly be a reference to ceremonial anointing. On the other hand, James may have had in mind medical treatment of believers physically bruised and battered by persecution. Perhaps it is better to understand the anointing in a metaphorical sense, representing the elders' work in encouraging, comforting, and strengthening the believer.

Unleashing the Text

Read James 5:13–20, noting the key words and definitions next to the passage.

suffering (v. 13)—The antidote to the suffering caused by evil treatment or persecution is seeking God's comfort through prayer.

James 5:13–20 (NKJV)

13 *Is anyone among you suffering? Let him pray. Is anyone cheerful? Let him sing psalms.*

Let him sing psalms. (v. 13)—The natural response of a joyful heart is to sing praise to God.

14 *Is anyone among you sick? Let him call for the elders of the church, and let them pray over him, anointing him with oil in the name of the Lord.*

15 *And the prayer of faith will save the sick, and the Lord will raise him up. And if he has committed sins, he will be forgiven.*

16 *Confess your trespasses to one another, and pray for one another, that you may be healed. The effective, fervent prayer of a righteous man avails much.*

17 *Elijah was a man with a nature like ours, and he prayed earnestly that it would not rain; and it did not rain on the land for three years and six months.*

18 *And he prayed again, and the heaven gave rain, and the earth produced its fruit.*

19 *Brethren, if anyone among you wanders from the truth, and someone turns him back,*

20 *let him know that he who turns a sinner from the error of his way will save a soul from death and cover a multitude of sins.*

sick (vv. 14–15)—James directs those who are "sick," meaning weakened by their suffering, to call for the elders of the church for strength, support, and prayer.

prayer of faith (v. 15)—the prayer offered on their behalf by the elders

save the sick (v. 15)—deliver them from their suffering because they have been weakened by their infirmity, not from their sin, which was confessed

committed sins . . . be forgiven (v. 15)—not by the elders, since God alone can forgive sins. That those who are suffering called for the elders implies they had a contrite, repentant heart, and that part of their time with the overseers would involve confessing their sins to God.

Confess your trespasses (v. 16)—Mutual honesty, openness, and sharing of needs will enable believers to uphold each other in the spiritual struggle.

The effective . . . avails much (v. 16)—The energetic, passionate prayers of godly men have the power to accomplish much.

Elijah . . . prayed . . . he prayed again (vv. 17–18)—Elijah provides one of the most notable illustrations of the power of prayer in the Old Testament. His prayers (not mentioned in the Old Testament account) both initiated and ended a three-and-a-half-year drought.

if anyone among you (v. 19)—This introduces a third category of people in the church (see vv. 13–14)—those professing believers who have strayed from the truth.

wanders from the truth (v. 19)— to apostatize from the faith he or she once professed. Such people are in grave danger (v. 20), and the church must call them back to the true faith.

sinner (v. 20)—a word used to describe the unregenerate (see James 4:8). James has in mind here those with dead faith (see 2:14–26), not true believers who sin.

the error of his way (v. 20)—Those who go astray doctrinally (v. 19) will also manifest an errant lifestyle, one not lived according to biblical principles.

save a soul from death (v. 20)—A person who wanders from the truth puts his soul in jeopardy. The "death" in view is not physical death, but eternal death—eternal separation from God and eternal punishment in hell. Knowing how high the stakes are should motivate Christians to aggressively pursue such people.

cover a multitude of sins (v. 20)—Since even one sin is enough to condemn a person to hell, James's use of the word "multitude" emphasizes the hopeless condition of lost, unregenerate sinners. The good news of the gospel is that God's forgiving grace (which is greater than any sin; Rom. 5:20) is available to those who turn from their sins and exercise faith in the Lord Jesus Christ (Eph. 2:8–9).

1) What kind of suffering does James refer to in verse 13? Is the context speaking of physical sickness or spiritual weakness? How do you know?

_____

_____

_____

2) How can prayer make a real difference in the life of a struggling saint?

_____

_____

_____

(Verses to consider: Ps. 27:13–14; Jon. 2:7; Phil. 4:6–7; 1 Pet. 5:7)

3) What do you learn from Elijah's example of faithful praying?

_____

_____

_____

(Verses to consider: 1 Kings 17:1–7; 18:1–2; 41–46)

4) What does it mean to "wander from the truth"?

_____

_____

_____

(Verses to consider: Heb. 5:12–6:9; 1 John 2:19)

5) To what group does James give the label "sinner" (v. 20)?

_____

_____

_____

GOING DEEPER

James was concerned about Christians straying from the faith. For more insight, read Jesus' parable in Matthew 13:24–30, 36–43.

24 *The kingdom of heaven is like a man who sowed good seed in his field;*

25 *but while men slept, his enemy came and sowed tares among the wheat and went his way.*

26 *But when the grain had sprouted and produced a crop, then the tares also appeared.*

27 *So the servants of the owner came and said to him, "Sir, did you not sow good seed in your field? How then does it have tares?"*

28 *He said to them, "An enemy has done this." The servants said to him, "Do you want us then to go and gather them up?"*

29 *But he said, "No, lest while you gather up the tares you also uproot the wheat with them.*

30 *Let both grow together until the harvest, and at the time of harvest I will say to the reapers, "First gather together the tares and bind them in bundles to burn them, but gather the wheat into my barn." . . .*

36 *Then Jesus sent the multitude away and went into the house. And His disciples came to Him, saying, "Explain to us the parable of the tares of the field."*

37 *He answered and said to them: "He who sows the good seed is the Son of Man.*

38 *The field is the world, the good seeds are the sons of the kingdom, but the tares are the sons of the wicked one.*

39 *The enemy who sowed them is the devil, the harvest is the end of the age, and the reapers are the angels.*

40 *Therefore as the tares are gathered and burned in the fire, so it will be at the end of this age.*

41 *The Son of Man will send out His angels, and they will gather out of His kingdom all things that offend, and those who practice lawlessness,*

42 *and will cast them into the furnace of fire. There will be wailing and gnashing of teeth.*

43 *Then the righteous will shine forth as the sun in the kingdom of their Father. He who has ears to hear, let him hear!"*

EXPLORING THE MEANING

6) According to this parable, what is at least one cause of people wandering from the faith?

_____

_____

_____

_____

_____

7) What does this parable add to your understanding of James's teaching on the danger of wandering from the truth? What are the consequences?

_____

_____

_____

_____

_____

(Verses to consider: Isa. 66:24; Dan. 2:2; Matt. 13:40, 42, 50;
Mark 9:43–49; Rom. 6:23; 2 Thess. 1:8–9; Rev. 20:11–15)

8) Read Acts 3:19. What does this teach about the necessity of sinners turning from sin? Salvation requires what?

_____

_____

_____

_____

(Verses to consider: Matt. 8:3; Luke 1:16–17; Acts 9:35; 2 Cor. 3:16; 1 Pet. 2:25)

TRUTH FOR TODAY

Maintaining open, sharing, and praying relationships with other Christians will help stop believers from bottoming out in their spiritual lives. Such relationships help give the spiritual strength that provides victory over sin. And they also provide godly pressure to confess and forsake sins before they become overwhelming to the point of total spiritual defeat.

God has granted to all believers the ministry of reconciling wandering souls to Himself. When the evidence indicates a professed believer's faith is not real, true Christians, knowing the terrible threat of eternal death that person faces, must make it their goal to turn him back from his sin to genuine saving faith in God.

REFLECTING ON THE TEXT

9) We can't pray for each other if we don't share our struggles and needs. Are you part of a small Bible study group or involved with another group of believers where you can share your heart? If not, why not?

_____

_____

_____

_____

_____

10) Are you spiritually defeated or discouraged right now? Make a list of fellow Christians (don't forget your church leaders!) from whom you could solicit prayer support. Before another day passes, contact these folks and share your situation and needs with them.

_____

_____

_____

_____

_____

11) Can you think of some professing believers in your church who, according to the tests of true faith found here in James, may not be actually saved? Pray for them right now.

_____

_____

_____

_____

_____

12) As we come to the end the book of James, what core truths will you take away from this study?

_____

_____

_____

_____

_____

PERSONAL RESPONSE

Write out additional reflections, questions you may have, or a prayer.

_____

_____

_____

_____

_____

_____

_____

_____

_____

_____

_____

_____

_____

_____

Additional Notes

Additional Notes

ADDITIONAL NOTES

Additional Notes

ADDITIONAL NOTES

ADDITIONAL NOTES

ADDITIONAL NOTES

Additional Notes

ADDITIONAL NOTES

ADDITIONAL NOTES

Additional Notes

Look for these exciting titles by John MacArthur

Experiencing the Passion of Christ

Experiencing the Passion of Christ Student Edition

Twelve Extraordinary Women Workbook

Twelve Ordinary Men Workbook

Welcome to the Family:
What to Expect Now That You're a Christian

What the Bible Says About Parenting:
Biblical Principles for Raising Godly Children

Hard to Believe Workbook:
The High Cost and Infinite Value of Following Jesus

The John MacArthur Study Library for PDA

The MacArthur Bible Commentary

The MacArthur Study Bible, NKJV

The MacArthur Topical Bible, NKJV

The MacArthur Bible Commentary

The MacArthur Bible Handbook

The MacArthur Bible Studies series